REVISE
English and
English Literature
Anthology for AQA A

Tony Childs

Heinemann

Published by Heinemann Educational Publishers
Hailey Court, Jordan Hill, Oxford OX2 8EJ
A part of Harcourt Education Limited

Reprinted 2004 (twice)

06 05 04
10 9 8 7 6 5 4

ISBN: 0 435 10288 5

Acknowledgements
Every effort has been made to contact copyright holders of material
reproduced in this book. Any omissions will be rectified in subsequent
printings if notice is given to the publishers.
Support material relating to works by Seamus Heaney and Simon Armitage,
printed with permission of Faber and Faber Limited; Support material
relating to works by Gillian Clarke, printed with permission of Carcanet
Press Limited; Support material relating to Carol Ann Duffy, printed with
permission of Anvil Press Poetry and Macmillan Publishers Limited.

Cover design by Hicks Design

Photographs: Kamau Brathwaite – WE Press/Chris Funkhouse; Tatamkhulu
Afrika – I-Africa; Grace Nichols – Sheila Geraghty/Penguin; Imtiaz Dharker
– Bloodaxe Books; Lawrence Ferlinghetti – Corbis/Lawrence Ferlinghetti;
Nissim Ezekiel – Images of India; Chinua Achebe – Heinemann
International; Denise Levertov – Associated Press; Sujata Bhatt –
Carcanet; Tom Leonard – Random House; John Agard – Penguin; Derek
Walcott – Corbis/Rune Hellestad; Niyi Osundare – Niyi Osundare; Moniza
Alvi – Oxford University Press; Seamus Heaney – Corbis Sygma/Richard
Frank Smith; Gillian Clarke – Carcanet Press; Carol Ann Duffy – Penguin
UK; Simon Armitage – Faber & Faber/Jason Bell; Doris Lessing – Corbis;
Sylvia Plath – Faber & Faber/Rollie McKenna; Michèle Roberts -
Camerapress/Nigel Hinkes; Joyce Cary – Corbis/Hulton Deutsch; Ernest
Hemingway – Corbis; Graham Swift – Corbis; Leslie Norris – John P. Snyder.

Produced by Gecko Ltd, Bicester, Oxon

Printed and bound in the UK by Biddles Ltd

Tel: 01865 888058 www.heinemann.co.uk

Contents

Contents

Introduction

About this book

This book is for GCSE students who are going to sit the AQA Specification A examinations in English and English Literature. The book is about the *AQA Anthology for Specification A*, which is the text for the study of poetry from Different Cultures and Traditions in English, and for the study of Pre-1914 and Post-1914 poetry in English Literature. The Prose section of the *Anthology*, which is one of the choices for Post-1914 prose in the Literature examination, is also covered in this book.

The book acts as a revision guide and as a self-study aid. Most of you are likely to have studied the *Anthology* material in class, with your teachers. Working through the relevant sections in this book will help to consolidate the work done in class, and to provide a springboard for tackling the examination itself with confidence. Some of you may be working independently or at home. You can use this book to select the best sections to study, and to prepare thoroughly for the examination.

The main sections of the book are designed to take you through all the poems and short stories in the *Anthology*. Following the questions and suggestions carefully will help you to explore and understand the pieces.

There are sample questions for both Foundation and Higher Tier candidates on all the English and English Literature categories, following the work on the individual pieces. They are written in the same style and at the same level as the questions in the AQA A examinations. There are also some suggestions for comparing poems and short stories.

The book also outlines how the *Anthology* fits into the English and English Literature courses, indicates what examiners are looking for in your answers, and gives advice on how to revise and how to tackle the examinations, including some suggestions about how you might structure and detail responses to a sample question in each category. At the back of the book there are sample answers to an examination question, with an examiner's comments showing how the answers would be assessed.

How to use this book to help you

In order to approach your exams with confidence, you need to understand what the writers of the pieces you have studied are saying, and how they say it. Then you need to be able to draw on that knowledge in the examination to answer the questions quickly and effectively. Because this is an 'open book' examination – that is to say, you can take your texts in with you – you have access to the texts in the *Anthology* in the exam to remind yourself about them, but, to save you time, you should not have to rely on them. You need to know the texts well enough to plan and write responses to the questions without spending too much time looking at the *Anthology* again.

1 Approaching the texts through the questions in this book

About the author and glossary

Where it is helpful to know something about an author in order to understand a story or poem better, or to know the meanings of some of the words (if they are archaic, for instance, or belong to a particular dialect), this information has been given at the start of the section on that particular poem or story. Generally, however, the emphasis is on you finding out about the piece yourself through a series of structured questions.

Questions

Before you begin working through the questions, you should always read through the piece once to get a feel for it. It is vital to do this without any preconceptions, so that you begin to form your own response to it. If you are using the book as a revision aid, you should still do this to remind yourself of the text.

You can then start working through the questions. If you like, you can make notes in a separate notebook or on paper as you go; but simply thinking through the questions may well be enough if you are using the book for revision. The questions are designed to take you through the pieces in logical steps, getting you to think about what the writers are saying and how they are saying it. Sometimes 'logical' means going through the piece chronologically, from beginning to end, looking for things on the way, and seeing the developing structure. Sometimes you may be asked to take an overall view of some features of the text from the start.

Final thoughts

The Final thoughts section is important. It nearly always asks you to read the piece again, and poses a final, usually general, question. It is important because, having worked through the questions, your initial response may well have been modified in some way. A further reading will confirm what you have observed about the piece as a whole, and may lead to some fresh thoughts in light of what you have learnt.

2 Annotation

The AQA A instructions about annotation read as follows:

For the 2004 examination only, candidates' copies of the Anthology may be annotated. Annotation means brief handwritten marginal notes, underlinings, highlightings and vertical lines in the margin. Additional notes on loose, interleaved sheets of paper and / or prepared answers are not permitted. The prohibition against candidates taking loose interleaved sheets of paper into the examination includes 'Post-it' notes.

For the 2005 and subsequent examinations, copies of the Anthology (and other set texts) taken into the examination room must not be annotated.

Therefore, apart from those preparing for the 2004 examination, the comments below about annotation **only** apply to your copy of the *Anthology* that you work with during the course. In 2004 you will be able to take your annotated *Anthology* into the examination room with you as long as you abide by the limitations set out above. In subsequent years, you will have a clean copy for the examination.

What you can't do in 2004 should be quite clear; another way of thinking about it might be that you can't bring in lots of continuous writing. It would not help you anyway (remember that you will not know the questions before you go in), and if you attempt to do so, you may well be disqualified from the examination. So what can you do, and what is the best way to use annotation to help you in the exam and before it?

If you've been working on these materials in class, you may already have made some annotations, which is fine – the more you work on the texts the better! The questions in this book simply offer you some more ideas. Most of the questions ask you to look for something, or to think about something. They might be focusing on exploring meaning, on the way the piece is written, or on aspects of different cultures (in English). If the questions lead you to something new about the piece, you may want to indicate this on the *Anthology* page, so that you'll remember it when you come back to it, either in revision or in the examination – for 2004 only.

3 Points of comparison

After each section in this book, you'll find notes on the ways in which the texts might be compared. The exam question will ask you to compare texts, so it is useful and important to start thinking along these lines. Of course, the suggestions here are not the only ones. It is not possible to note down every way of looking at every possible combination of poems or stories, and anyway you don't know the questions before you go into the exam. It is better to think of these suggestions as examples of how you might compare the poems or stories.

4 Sample structures

At the end of the sections, you'll find examples of how a response to a particular question might be structured and detailed. Again, these are only suggestions – there are all sorts of ways of structuring responses, and you don't know the questions – but they will show you a method of organising your ideas so that you can show off your knowledge effectively.

5 The practice examination questions

Each short story and each poetry cluster is followed by practice examination questions; one for each tier. At the back of the book you will also find some sample examination answers, each with an examiner's commentary. Whether or not you actually try answering them (and if you do, the best thing is to give yourself the same time as you will have in the exam itself), you should look at these questions very carefully to see what sort of thing you will be expected to do. The question type and format are exactly the same as you will face in the examination. Even if you don't answer the questions in full, it will help you to make essay plans for each question.

Preparing for the examination

1 Revision

The texts

The most important thing to do is simply to *re-read the texts* themselves. This will help to make you more familiar with the details of each, so you don't need to look things up all the time during the exam. It will also help you to find new things. Even if you're in the last week before the examination, you should aim to to read all your chosen texts at least twice, recapping on the points you've picked up before.

Using this book

If you're using this book as a revision aid you may find that the questions seem to take you in a different direction from the one you took with your teachers. Don't worry about this! What the examiner is interested in is what **you** think, and the more different ways you look at a text, the more likely it is that you will come to a firm view of what you think about it. *What is important is that you can argue for your point of view, drawing on the text for evidence.*

Comparing poems and stories

All the exam questions will ask you to compare texts – one poem with another in English, and several poems together or one story with another in English Literature. It's important to think about this when revising too. The questions here on the poems and stories are designed to get you to think about individual texts, because there are any number of different ways in which they might be 'paired', and after all, knowing the texts is the most important thing. Nevertheless, the better you get to know them, the more likely you are to see similarities and differences between them, both in content and style, and you should consciously look for these comparisons after you've worked through all your texts for the first time.

> To summarise, you should:
> - read all your texts again in your revision period
> - work out your own point of view on each text, and be able to support it with evidence
> - remember that the questions will ask you to compare, and be prepared for any combination.

2 Sitting the examination

- First – don't forget to bring your texts with you!

- The next thing to do is to set about making good use of your time. In **English Paper 2** you have an hour and a half for the whole paper, and you are advised to spend about 45 minutes on Section A – the poetry from Different Cultures and Traditions. This reflects the marks available to you, so it's important to stick to this timing as closely as you can. When you attempt any of the practice questions, give yourself 45 minutes to plan, write and check – don't cheat!

  In the **English Literature exam**, you are advised to spend about 45 minutes of the 1 hour 45 minutes on the prose section, and an hour on the poetry. This reflects exactly the division of marks – 30 per cent of the total marks for English Literature are available for the prose section, and 40 per cent for the poetry. As with English, therefore, it's important to stick as closely as you can to this timetable.

  It is important not to start writing too quickly within the time you have for each question. Time for planning and thought is built into the timing of the exam – so use it!

- Making a good choice of question to tackle is vital. Give yourself the time to read your possible choices carefully. Look for the question you're happiest with in each section, either because it centres on the texts you want to write about, or because it asks an interesting question that you think you can write about well. When you've made your choice, read the question again very carefully, identifying exactly what the elements of the question are. After all, you've spent a lot of time reading the texts, so it's worth spending a little time reading what you're asked to do with them!

- Next, plan your answer. With the poetry question, you'll need to choose the poems that will fit best into your answer. You may choose simply to follow the prompts in the question, though as long as you tackle them all it doesn't matter how you fit them in. You must try to construct a logical order to your response, which allows you to answer the question. The sections in this book called **Structuring a response** may help you here. Telling the story is not the way to answer! You should be thinking about what the writer has to say, and how he or she says it.

- Now you can start writing. Remember what you've learned about the pieces, and to support what you say with references to the texts, and you'll be fine. Remember, too, that every question will ask you to write about how the writers have written, as well as what they have said.

Section 1
English

How the English Anthology fits into the course

The AQA A English course is assessed through a terminal examination, which counts for 60 per cent, and coursework, which counts for 40 per cent of the final mark. Reading response to poetry from Different Cultures and Traditions is assessed in English Paper 2 Section A, and is worth 15 per cent of the total mark.

In the paper, there is a choice of two questions. Each question will ask you to compare two poems from the Different Cultures and Traditions clusters in the *Anthology*. One poem in each question will be named, and you can choose which other poem to use in response to the question. You will be advised to spend about 45 minutes on your answer to this question.

What the examiners are looking for

The Assessment Objectives

The Assessment Objectives for any examination specification show what candidates have to do in their examinations for that specification. Examiners have to decide how well individual candidates have fulfilled these objectives in their examination performance, and give marks accordingly.

Here are the Assessment Objectives for GCSE English Reading which are tested in Paper 2 Section A. Candidates must demonstrate their ability to:

1 **Read, with insight and engagement, making appropriate references to texts and developing and sustaining interpretations of them.**
This means that you have to show that you understand the poems you've read – that you've come to an 'interpretation' of them, that you can explain what you think about them, and that you can provide evidence for the examiner of your reasons for thinking what you do. This means that you have to make 'appropriate references to texts', through quotations or other means of showing your knowledge. The more detailed and organised you can be in your response, the better.

2 **Select material appropriate to their purpose, collate material from different sources, and make cross references.**
This means that you have to compare one poem with another in the examination. You will have to choose a poem that is suitable to compare with the named poem, then find appropriate features from each to compare, or 'cross-reference', in response to the question. Of course, you can choose any poem to compare with the named poem, and there will therefore be any number of ways to compare. This book will offer you some ways to think about comparison, and an example of how to structure a response.

3 **Understand and evaluate how writers use linguistic, structural and presentational devices to achieve their effects, and comment on ways language varies and changes.**
This means that you have to show that you understand how the writers of the poems use language and structure, and various ways of presenting their ideas, in their work. Your knowledge of these features has to be linked to 'effects' – how the features work in affecting your response to the poems. Of course, you have to

provide evidence for your knowledge – see point 2. There are considerable variations in the language of the poems in the clusters, of course, reflecting the different cultures and traditions they are drawn from, and you will be tested on your knowledge of these too.

What the examiners will expect to see

The questions on the examination paper will be designed to test how well the candidates can fulfil the Assessment Objectives through writing about the poems in response to the questions. So what will they expect to see?

Simply, they will want to see that you know the poems, and can think about them. *Knowing your texts* means not only being familiar with the details, but also understanding what they mean (in your view) and how they're written, and being able to move around them confidently to support what you have to say, without necessarily having to look them up all the time! Don't rely on having your *Anthology* with you in the examination – you should know the poems well enough before you go into the examination to spend nearly all of your time thinking about the question and writing your response. You should only have to look at the *Anthology* to check details if necessary.

Thinking about the poems means showing your opinions and understanding of the poems in response to the questions you have been asked. This may seem very obvious – but often candidates will try to write down everything they know about a poem rather than answering the question, hoping that some of it will be relevant. A vital stage in thinking is to plan a response in the light of the question you've chosen to respond to. Look very carefully at the key words of the task, and decide what you're going to say and use, and in what order, so that you can produce the most effective response. That's why learning an 'answer' before you go into the exam is never the best thing to do – after all, you don't know what the question will be! Go into the exam knowing the poems, and respond directly to the question.

Kamau Brathwaite

a — Kamau Brathwaite is a Barbadian poet, historian and essayist.

Limbo

g

Glossary

limbo — a West Indian dance that involves bending over backwards and passing under a horizontal stick

slave ships — An estimated 15 million Africans were transported to the Americas between 1540 and 1850. Chained together by their hands and feet, the slaves had little room to move. A large number of slaves died in transit, and many were crippled for life as a consequence of the way they were chained up on the ship.

Read and revise

The poet has chosen the words and rhythm of a dance – the limbo – in this poem. Read it through once (preferably aloud), listening to the rhythm as it repeats and shifts.

1 Some words in the poem are in italics. Which words? Why are they repeated?

2 How does the poet set up this refrain, and its rhythm, at the beginning of the poem? Look at lines 2–6.

3 The rhythm of the lines that are not italicised varies throughout the poem in an intricate pattern – like dance steps. Look at line 7 ('long dark night is the silence in front of me') and work out the rhythm in your head – it's a bit like a syncopated rap. Now look through the poem, finding as many variations on the rhythm of this line as you can. Sometimes you'll find repetitions, and sometimes the rhythm is broken up over two or more lines.

4 The limbo is a dance that flows continuously. Find the first full stop in the poem.

5 Now look at the first two lines, where both rhythms are introduced to the reader. The first line isn't quite right, though – which is the extra word? Why do you think the poet makes the unusual choice of beginning with a conjunction – 'and'? You might think about Question 4.

6 In the limbo, the dancer starts with the stick in front of him, goes down under it, and comes up on the other side. The prepositions 'in front of', 'down', 'under', 'up', and 'on' trace this movement. Pick out the prepositions in the poem which trace the same movement, beginning with 'the silence in front of me' (line 1).

7 Now begin to trace the story that is told through the words and rhythm of the song. The progress of the limbo dance is compared to the voyage across the ocean. When the slave is brought on board the ship, what is 'in front of him', like the limbo stick? Why is it also like a 'long dark night', do you think?

8 Look at lines 10–14.

- The triple beat of 'stick hit sound' is very strong here. How does the poet make it seem strong? Think about repetition, and where the poet has chosen to break the line.

- There's another sound repeated here, to emphasise the beat. Which words rhyme?

- Why do you think the poet has chosen to make the beat so strong here? Think about 'stick hit', and what might be happening on the ship.

- Which stage of the ship's voyage is being described here? Which words tell you, and how are they linked?

9 Look at lines 16 and 17. Which words here are repeated from earlier in the poem to capture the sense of the dance continuing, but unfolding?

10 Look at lines 20–23.

- If the 'stick' of the limbo represents things that the dancer has to survive, what does he have to survive here? What does the ship represent?

- Lines 20 and 21 are repeated exactly, unlike any other repetitions, apart from the refrain. Why, do you think? What is the poet trying to reinforce here?

11 By line 27, where is the speaker exactly, in relation to the limbo stick and the ship? Find the exact point later on in the poem where his situation changes.

12 'Knees spread wide' (line 28) clearly shows where the speaker is in relation to the stick – where might he be in the ship, where he is forced to be in this uncomfortable position? Line 21 tells you where he is in the ship, too.

13 Look at lines 34–36, 'down / down / down'.

- There are several lines in the poem with three strong beats – line 10, for example. Here, though, the words (and beats) have been split over three lines. Why, do you think?

- Where is this pattern both repeated and reversed? Think what is described in between. Perhaps this is the key moment of the dance – how is it the key part of the voyage?

14 Look carefully at lines 37–43. Although the dancer is going under the stick here, there are clear indications of success.

- What does the limbo drum beat appear to be doing, in the speaker's mind?

- What change is marked by the first word in line 40? How is this different from what has gone before? What does it seem to suggest?

- How does line 41 imply success?

- How do lines 42 and 43 reinforce the idea in line 40, and imply success in the dance very strongly?

15 More is being suggested than just success in the dance. The 'gods' (line 43) are raising him and the music 'saving me' (line 47). In relation to the voyage, why might the speaker be thinking in this way?

16 Now look at the last four lines, which bring the poem to a rather unexpected conclusion.

- Three words (and beats) spread over three lines have been seen before – but these are different. How? Compare them to the other examples in the poem.

- 'Step' implies progress, moving forward – but this is 'hot' and 'slow'. Why, do you think? Think about the nature of the life that faces the slave who has survived the voyage.

- There is a progression about light and heat in the last 11 lines, from 'sun' to 'hot' to 'burning'. Why do you think this ground is 'burning'? Think about what the 'burning ground' might do to the feet that 'step' on it, and think again about the place.

- There is only one full stop in the poem: at the end. What other reason might there be for a full stop here, apart from it being the end of the poem? What full stop has been reached?

17 The limbo runs through the poem, but the last refrain appears in lines 38 and 39. Why does the poet choose not to repeat the refrain at the end, do you think?

Final thoughts

As you have seen, the poem depends on the rhythm of the dance – including the sudden loss of rhythm in the last line. Read the poem through again, listening to the rhythms and getting the story clear in your head.

Comparisons

You might compare this poem with:

- Nothing's Changed / Presents from My Aunts . . . (identity)
- What Were They Like? (unusual presentation)
- Presents from my Aunts . . . / What Were They Like? (specific cultural references)
- Island Man / Half-Caste (non-standard English)
- Night of the Scorpion / What Were They Like? (traditions)

Tatamkhulu Afrika

a

Tatmkhulu Afrika was born in Egypt, but has spent most of his life in South Africa. He spent many years actively opposing the apartheid system in South Africa, which was imposed by the white government. White and black South Africans were kept apart by law, and the black population was denied political power and representation, and many civic rights.

Nothing's Changed

g

Glossary

District Six	a residential area of Cape Town, South Africa
brash	offensively 'showy'
incipient	developing, just starting
Port Jackson	large pine trees, introduced to South Africa from Australia
bunny chows	cheap South African take-away food

Read and revise

The strongest impact of this poem probably depends on 'Nothing's changed', which is both the title and the last line. Read the poem right through once, with the title in mind.

1 The poem is divided into stanzas of irregular lengths, though most have eight lines. Which stanza stands out as being furthest from the eight line pattern?

2 The speaker is identified by 'I' (or 'my') in several stanzas. In one stanza the second person 'you' is used – which one? Only one stanza has 'we', and the word is repeated in the same line – find it.

3 Which stanza has been signposted by structure and language as a key stanza?

4 The first stanza is one long, continuous sentence, ending with the full stop at the end of line 8.

- The sentence gives a feeling of drifting. How does the poet achieve this? Think about the number of commas, and the number of things mentioned.

- There is a sense of direction, nevertheless. What do the verbs tell you? Notice where they are placed on the line, too.

- Having read the whole poem, does this strike you as a black or white approach to the location of the poem? Why?

5 Look at the second stanza (lines 9–16), which begins the emotional story of the poem.

- The first line is unusual in the poem – there's a full stop at the end of the line, and no verb. Why do you think the poet has created this rather bald line?

- Which line reminds the reader (and the speaker) that 'nothing's changed'?

- Lines 12–15 form a list. How does the poet draw your attention to the fact that it is a list? Think about placement of words in the line.

- Why do you think these things are important to the speaker? Why does the poet want to draw your attention to these things?

- What emotion does the speaker feel? How does the poet draw your attention to it? Think about where the word that tells you what he is feeling comes in the sentence, and in the line.

6 The third stanza (lines 17–24) describes the inn, apparently without emotion. This is the only stanza without a personal pronoun, which makes it seem objective – but it isn't really.

- This is all one sentence, but the poet has shaped it so that it begins 'Brash with glass'. Why do you think the poet has done this? Think about the impact of the first word and phrase on the reader.

- The name is 'flaring like a flag' (line 18). The poet draws attention to 'flag' by using **alliteration** – the repetition of a consonant sound to gain effect. Which sound is repeated? What do you think the name is a 'flag' of?

- Line 19 only has two words, emphasising the word 'squats', especially as the reader has to break slightly before the next word. Why do you think the poet has chosen this word to describe where the inn is?

- Are there any words in lines 20–24 which might also affect the reader? Remember the tone that the poet has established about this place.

7 Lines 25 and 26 form a key moment in the poem (see Questions 1–3).

- Line 25 is almost a repetition of a previous line – find it. How has 'nothing changed'?

- 'No sign says it is' means 'is whites only'. It would be natural for this to follow straight on from line 24 – why do you think the poet has chosen not to do this?

- The personal 'my' now becomes 'we' (line 26). Who are 'we', do you think? Where do 'we' belong? (Think about the following two lines.) Why do you think the speaker has chosen to widen the poem's statement to include others? How has 'nothing changed'?

8 In lines 27–32, how has 'nothing changed', and which phrase tells you that the speaker knows that nothing has changed?

9 Lines 33–40 form a sharp contrast with what has gone before. Pick out all the words and phrases which contrast with the picture drawn of the inn, in lines 22–3 and 30–32. Think about choices of language as well as the things described.

10 The poet's choices of structure and language create a sense of belonging together in this stanza. The two sentences are not separated into different stanzas, and the second person, 'you', creates a sense of belonging too. How else does the poet make this place seem more human than the inn?

11 The stanza ends with 'it's in the bone' (line 40). What do you think this means? Think about the title again.

12 How does the poet show in lines 41–44 that the speaker feels small and rejected? Think about the effect of the two words in line 42, and the comma in line 44, as well as the meaning of the words.

13 The word 'burn' (line 45) is emphasised by being placed at the end of a two-word line, before the reader has to break slightly. How does the word contrast with the scene inside the glass? Think about lines 30–32. How else is 'burn' a good choice of word? Think about what the speaker is feeling, and what he would like to do.

14 How has 'nothing changed' (line 48)? Think about both sides of this divide.

Final thoughts

The final line brings the poem full circle, back to the beginning – the title. How does this choice of structure fit the meaning of the poem?

Comparisons

You might compare this poem with:

- Limbo / *from* Search For My Tongue (identity)
- This Room / What Were They Like? (change)
- Two Scavengers in a Truck . . . / Vultures (politics)
- Night of the Scorpion / Not My Business (first person)
- Two Scavengers in a Truck . . . / Limbo (cultural references)
- Two Scavengers in a Truck . . . / Hurricane Hits England (particular places)
- Vultures / Love After Love (universal idea)

Grace Nichols

a Grace Nichols was born and educated in Guyana in the West Indies. She came to Britain in 1977.

Island Man

Read and revise

The poem presents two contrasting pictures – the Caribbean island in the man's head, and the reality of his surroundings. The poet has made some unusual choices of structure and language to show this contrast. Read the poem through once, noticing some of the unusual positions of words on lines.

1 The poem has no punctuation at all. Why do you think the poet has chosen to do this? Think about the scene that is in the island man's head.

2 Although there is no punctuation, the poet does use capital letters – but not many. Look at the capital letters in the poem, and try to decide why the poet has used them at these points. Notice that there are more in the second half of the poem than the first. Why, do you think? Think about the formality of capital letters in the context of this poem.

3 The dedication under the title is in italics, unlike the rest of the poem. Why, do you think? How is the language of the dedication different from the language of the rest of the poem? Why?

4 The poem presents two pictures, but the distinction between the two is not sharp – because it only gradually becomes clear in the man's head. Try to identify exactly where the change comes – and notice how the unusually placed words are in the same part of the poem.

5 The words used in the first half of the poem, describing the island, contrast strongly with those in the second, describing London. Find as many contrasts as you can. Look for colours; sights and sounds; natural and artificial features.

6 The first line is the only one that consists of a single word. Why do you think the poet has chosen to do this?

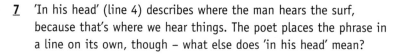

7 'In his head' (line 4) describes where the man hears the surf, because that's where we hear things. The poet places the phrase in a line on its own, though – what else does 'in his head' mean?

8 What do you think 'wombing' (line 5) means? Think about where the man comes from, and what has just happened to him. You might think of the sound of the words, too, and the sound of the surf. (When the sound of a word matches the sound of the thing being described, it is called **onomatopoeia**.)

9 Why do you think the sun is described as coming up 'defiantly' (line 8)?

10 The first unusually placed words occur in line 11 – 'groggily groggily'. Clearly the gaps created as you read this line and the next line (after the stanza break) create the sense of struggle as the man wakes up. Can you think of any other effect created by these two words, and where they are placed? Think about what else is 'misplaced' in the poem.

11 Line 12 begins with a capital letter – why, do you think? Is this a new beginning, or not?

12 The island and the city are mixed up – confused, almost – in the man's head as he wakes up in lines 12–14.

- Which words suggest nature and the island in these lines, and which words suggest the city?

- The gap created after 'soar' by the placing of 'to surge of wheels' at the end of line 14 causes a sense of expectation about what might come next. Which word in line 14 indicates the reality? Notice where the word comes in the line.

13 Line 15 belongs almost completely to the city – but what does the word 'roar' still connect with? Remember that rhyme connects things.

14 'Muffling muffling' (line 16) is the second time a word has been repeated. Where was the first? What do both repetitions describe about what is going on in the man's head? How is the sound of the traffic 'muffling' what is in his head?

15 What are the 'crumpled pillow waves', do you think? Think about the sounds in the man's head, and when he has heard them. Think about the physical appearance of the pillow, too.

16 It is an effort for the island man to come back to reality. How is this effort conveyed?

17 Look carefully at the last line.

- The last line is broken off from the rest of the poem – it is the only line that stands by itself. Why do you think the poet has made this structural choice? Think about the nature of the statement, and what has gone before.

- This is the only line in the poem with two words with capital letters. Why has the poet made this choice, do you think? Think about the nature of London life.

Final thoughts

Read the whole poem again, thinking about the movement in the island man's head from the island to London. What does the last, isolated line show about the progress of the movement?

Comparisons

You could compare this poem with:

- Presents from my Aunts . . . / Hurricane Hits England (people)

- Limbo / Half-Caste (non-standard English)

- Presents from my Aunts . . . / *from* Search For My Tongue (two cultures)

- What Were They Like? (loss of culture)

- Limbo (transition between places)

Imtiaz Dharker

a — Imtiaz Dharker lives in Bombay in India.

Blessing

Read and revise

Read the poem through once, to get the shape of it. Notice particularly the changing length of sentences.

<u>1</u> Count the number of lines that each sentence takes. You'll see that the second half of the poem forms one long sentence. Why do you think the poet chooses to do this? Think what the last sentence is about.

<u>2</u> The poem is divided into stanzas of different lengths, reflecting different stages of the story in the poem.

<u>3</u> What sort of community is the poem set in? Look carefully through the poem for any indications you can find. Think about what people have, what they might believe, what is around them.

<u>4</u> Look at the first stanza (lines 1 and 2), which gives the situation in the poem.

- The stanza consists of two **end-stopped lines** – lines with a full stop at the end. Why do you think the poet has chosen to start with two short sentences? The second sentence states a simple fact, and stops. Why?

- Skin is described as cracking 'like a pod'. Why, do you think? Think about appearance, and any other associations the word 'pod' might have.

<u>5</u> Now look at the second stanza (lines 3–6).

- What is this stanza about? Think about the key word that the poet has chosen, and where he has placed it.

- This is a four line sentence, which repeats itself by mentioning the same thing in a number of ways. Why has the poet formed a longer sentence here? What do the repetitions show about the state of mind of the people in the community? Remember the key word.

- What is being imagined, exactly – sight or sound? How many?

- The sounds in the imagination amount to 'the voice of a kindly god'. Why would this be a 'kindly' god? Remember what the title of the poem is.

6 Look at lines 7–9, which describe the event that shapes the rest of the poem.

- 'Fortune' (line 8) means 'luck', which the event is, but it means something else too. Connect the word 'fortune' with a word in line 9.

- What do you think is the 'silver' that 'crashes to the ground'? If it is water, how does this make sense of line 7?

7 The sounds imagined in the second stanza are all small. Which word in line 11 indicates a much greater sound?

8 In lines 11–17, there are a lot of indications of the size of the response to the water. Find as many as you can. Look for:
- words that suggest numbers of people
- words that suggest different people
- words that suggest a variety of things.

9 One of the words that you've picked out for Question 8 suggests a religious gathering. Which one? Why has the poet used this particular word?

10 Why do you think the poet has chosen not to put commas between the words 'man woman child'? Think about Question 8.

11 Why are the hands 'frantic' (line 17), do you think? Think about numbers again, and what people are feeling.

12 The final stanza (lines 18–23) deals with the aftermath of the event.

- Pick out the words in this stanza that refer to sound. What sort of sounds are these? How have they changed from earlier in the poem?

- Which words in the stanza suggest that things have improved from the beginning of the poem?

- Which words here connect with 'the voice of a kindly god' (line 6)? How do you know that the poet wants you to think about this element of the poem?

- The blessing sings 'over their small bones'. What is it that is going 'over their small bones'? If this is a 'blessing', what religious association might this have?

Final thoughts

Now you've worked through the poem, read it once more, registering the way that the sentence lengths and stanza divisions help the effect of the poem.

Comparisons

You might compare this poem with:

- Nothing's Changed (description)
- This Room (metaphor)
- Night of the Scorpion / What Were They Like? (particular cultures)

Lawrence Ferlinghetti

a Lawrence Ferlinghetti was born in New York in 1919, and became one of the Beat generation of poets in the 1950s. He was one of the most political of the Beats.

Two Scavengers in a Truck, Two Beautiful People in a Mercedes

g

Glossary	
stoop	rear footplate
coifed	styled
gargoyle	a grotesque figure
Quasimodo	the name of the Hunchback of Nôtre Dame

Read and revise

Read the poem right through once. The poem builds up a picture piece by piece – notice how it keeps adding details.

<u>1</u> The layout of this poem is unusual – the lines begin at the beginning of the line, or centred, or to the right, without a clear pattern. What effect does this have on the way you read it? Think about the pauses you have to make.

<u>2</u> How many main verbs are there in these 37 lines? How many actions are there?

<u>3</u> How many full stops has the poet used?

<u>4</u> Looking at your answers to Questions 1, 2 and 3 together, how has the poet used structure and language to create a picture of a moment, adding one detail after another, rather than a story in which a number of things happen?

<u>5</u> Although there are no full stops, there are some capital letters. Find all of them, and notice what sorts of words have capitals, and where they appear. How do they add to the sense of details being added one by one, without anything happening?

<u>6</u> The first two lines set the time and place for the picture. Notice which word the poet has chosen to be the first read. How does it suggest that this is a 'still' picture, rather than something moving?

7 Read to the end of line 9, 'with an elegant couple in it'. The word 'elegant' is emphasised by being repeated in lines 8 and 9. The repetition also invites the reader to compare the couple with the two garbagemen. In the poem so far, what details suggest differences between the two pairs of people? Look carefully at all the words, including the title.

8 Now read lines 10–15, which add more details about the people in the Mercedes. Line 9 describes them as 'an elegant couple'. Which details in these lines add to the idea of them being 'elegant', or 'beautiful', as the title suggests? How are these two people similar?

9 The first break in the poem – a blank line between stanzas – comes between lines 15 and 16. Find the next break. What does the stanza defined by the breaks, from line 16 onwards, describe?

10 Which details in the description of the two 'scavengers' contrast with the people in the Mercedes? Look for words and phrases, and think about their effect.

11 Lines 23–25 suggest that one of the men is similar to the Mercedes driver. How is he similar? How is he different? Why do you think the poet has chosen to mention this similarity? Think about line 32, and what the whole poem might mean.

12 Look at the next stanza (lines 26–30).

- How does the poet emphasise how far apart the scavengers and the 'cool couple' are?

- The TV ad, which the couple might represent for the scavengers, is described as 'odorless', which is an unusual choice of word to use to describe an advert. Why does the poet use this word?

13 Now look at the last stanza (lines 31–37).

- Line 31 defines how long this picture lasts. Which phrase defines it? Why do you think the poet makes it clear that the moment is so short?

- The idea of 'anything' or 'everything' being possible occurs in line 30, and again in line 33. Which words in line 33 suggest that perhaps this isn't true?

- In lines 35 and 36, how does the poet suggest that the distance between the two couples is really very great, and difficult to cross?

- The poet has chosen 'democracy' as the last word of the poem. Work out how the pattern of the last three lines leads up to this word. Think about their appearance on the page.

- The fact that 'democracy' is the last word in the poem suggests that it is important to the poem; it is also the only abstract word in the poem. In a democracy 'everything is always possible'. How does the poet suggest that perhaps this is not the case for the scavengers?

Final thoughts

Read the poem through again, noticing how all the details lead to the final thought, and word. What do you think the poem is about?

Comparisons

You might compare this poem with:
- Island Man / Half-Caste (people)
- Nothing's Changed / *from* Unrelated Incidents (politics)
- Nothing's Changed / Night of the Scorpion (specific cultural references)
- Nothing's Changed (particular place)
- Nothing's Changed / Vultures (universal idea)

Nissim Ezekiel

a | Nissim Ezekiel was born in 1924, and lives in Bombay in India. He is a Jew.

Night of the Scorpion

g

> **Glossary**
>
> **diabolic** — of the devil, fiendish
>
> **sceptic** — somebody who doubts religious ideas
>
> **rationalist** — somebody who relies on reason to make judgements, not belief

Read and revise

Read the whole poem through once, to take the story in. Try to decide why there is a line break before the last three lines.

1 This poem is set in a particular culture.

- Apart from religion, what can you find in the poem that helps to define the place where the people in the poem live?

- Now look for religious references. You should find at least eight, including people, practices and concepts.

2 Look again at lines 1–7, which tell you about the event that starts the action of the rest of the poem.

- 'I remember' sets the poem as a first person narrative, but for much of the poem it's easy to forget that this is a description of an event from the point of view of someone who witnessed it. Find the next line in the poem after 'I remember' which uses 'I'.

- Most of lines 1–7 are factual. Which word in line 6 is not? What does it suggest about the scorpion?

3 Now look again at lines 8–14, which describe the peasants.

- What are the peasants compared to in lines 8 and 9? Which words are used to compare them? Why do you think the poet makes this comparison?

- Why do you think the poet compares the shadows on the wall to 'giant scorpion shadows'? Think about the watcher – what he sees, how old he might be, what he is doing, what he imagines.

31

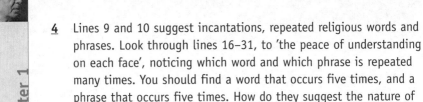

4 Lines 9 and 10 suggest incantations, repeated religious words and phrases. Look through lines 16–31, to 'the peace of understanding on each face', noticing which word and which phrase is repeated many times. You should find a word that occurs five times, and a phrase that occurs five times. How do they suggest the nature of the peasants' talk?

5 The word 'May' always occurs at the beginning of a line. Why do you think the poet has made this choice? Saying it aloud (or aloud in your head) may help you.

6 A number of ideas about birth, life and death are mentioned in lines 16–28. What do these ideas show about the beliefs of the peasants?

7 The peasants are described as having 'the peace of understanding' (line 31) on their faces. From the watching child's point of view, does this help the mother? Who is it about?

8 Lines 32–35 do not suggest 'peace'. How does the poet suggest what the watching child's feelings might be in these lines? Think about the effect of the repeated word, and words and phrases from which we can infer how he must be feeling.

9 How is the child's father shown to be desperate to help the mother in lines 36–40? Think about:
- what he does despite his beliefs
- the effect of the list in line 38
- the word which suggest desperation in line 39, as well as the action.

10 The words 'I watched' (line 41) are repeated in line 42. What is the poet reminding the reader of at this point? Why, do you think?

11 Which word in line 41 suggests what the child is feeling as he watches?

12 Lines 44 and 45 become factual again, like the first 7 lines. How does the poet show this simplicity? Think about the choice of breaking the line. How do these two lines feel like a conclusion?

13 Finally, look at the last three lines of the poem.
- 'Only' in line 46 is a simple word, but powerful here. How does 'only' contrast with what has happened, and been said, since she was stung? Think about the peasants (and the repeated phrase about them), the father, the holy man.

- The words of the poem are 'spoken' by the watching child. What do you think the word 'only' might reveal about the way the child felt about his mother at the time, and feels about her now?

- The mother is heard for the first time here. How do the mother's words contrast with what has gone before?

- The poet has chosen 'and spared my children' as the last line of the poem. This makes the reader think about her, and what her priorities are – and about somebody else too. What do you think the watcher will have thought and felt when she said this?

Final thoughts

Read the poem through again, concentrating on the watcher. Why do you think the child has remembered these things? Although the child seems absent for much of the poem, how has the poet reminded you that there is a watcher, who is closely involved?

Comparisons

You might compare this poem with:
- Presents from my Aunts ... / Island Man (people)
- Nothing's Changed / Presents from my Aunts ... (first person)
- Hurricane Hits England / Limbo (specific cultural references)
- Presents from my Aunts ... / What Were They Like? (traditions)

Chinua Achebe

a — Chinua Achebe was born in Ogidi, Nigeria, in 1930. He is a leading Nigerian novelist, and is regarded as one of the finest novelists writing in English.

Vultures

g —

Glossary

harbingers	things which warn of what is to come
charnel-house	a building in which bodies or bones are deposited
Belsen	a notorious concentration camp in World War II, where thousands of people were gassed
perpetuity	for ever

Read and revise

Read the poem through once, noticing how the poem is divided into four different sections.

1 Work out how the poet has marked the changes from one section to another. Think about:

- capital letters
- indentation
- ellipses, which is the name for lines of three dots (...).

2 The four sections reflect different stages of the argument of the poem. The first words of each section, though, set the intention of the section. Which word in line 30 shows that this is a stage of an argument? Which word in line 41 suggests an instruction, which is a result of the argument?

3 This element of the course is called Different Cultures and Traditions. There is more than one culture referred to here.

- Where do you think the setting for the first section of the poem is? Think about the creatures, and what is around them.

- Section three is clearly set in a different culture, and in the past – is there any indication of when the scene in the first section takes place?

- Why do you think the poet has chosen to refer to different cultures, and probably different times? Remember that this is a poem with a message. Who is the message for? What is it about? Is it just about one culture?

4 The first section of the poem defines the situation that the poet thinks about in the rest of the poem. Look at the first four lines, which define the time when the situation happens.

- The poet creates a dark, miserable tone here. How does he do this? Pick out all the words that help to create the tone.

- 'Unstirred by harbingers of sunbreak' means there is no sign of the sun. How does this add to the tone? How is it appropriate that this scene is set in near darkness? Think about the last two lines of the poem.

5 The rest of the first sentence, from 'a vulture' (line 4) to 'to hers' (line 13) describes the vultures.

- Look at the description of the tree (lines 5–6). How does this description fit the tone established so far, and the nature of the vultures themselves?

- How has the poet made the male vulture seem unattractive? Think about the words the poet uses to describe the vulture's head and feathers, and then the comparisons he makes.

- Pick out the words that suggest there is some warmth and love between the vultures. Look for more than one example.

6 Look at the rest of the first section, from 'Yesterday' (line 13) to 'telescopic eyes ... ' (line 21), which paints a very unattractive picture of the vultures.

- How has the poet made the vultures seem unattractive in these lines? Think about what they do, and the words the poet uses to describe them.

- How has the poet made their prey seem horrible?

7 Look back over your answers to Questions 4, 5 and 6. Which are the only words in the first section which stand out as being different?

8 Now look at the second section (lines 22–29), which moves the poem on.

- Line 22 is the only line in the poem that consists of a single word. Why do you think the poet has chosen to do this? Think about how the nature of the poem changes here, and the pauses created as you read.

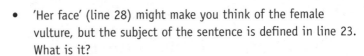

- 'Her face' (line 28) might make you think of the female vulture, but the subject of the sentence is defined in line 23. What is it?

- Love is personified here. **Personification** is an abstract idea – like love – being given human characteristics. What does 'love' do here, which is human?

- If 'her face' is the face of love, not the vulture's, has the thought in this verse anything to do with the vultures? Where is 'that charnel-house'?

<u>9</u> Now look at line 30, which starts to take the poem away from the vultures completely.

- The second section starts to generalise about love. When you read line 30, how do you know that the poet has continued to generalise and moved away from the situation of the vultures?

- How does the punctuation at the beginning of line 30 show that the thought in the second section is being developed here?

- Which word in line 30 belongs to the language of argument, or working things out?

<u>10</u> Now look at the rest of the third section, to 'Daddy's / return' (lines 39–40).

- Which words in lines 32–35 make the Commandant seem unattractive?

- Which words in lines 36–40 make the Commandant seem exactly the opposite to the person described in lines 32–35? Think about the associations of each word that you pick out.

<u>11</u> How is the situation described in the third section the same as the situation described in the first section, even though they are set in different places, cultures and times?

<u>12</u> Having described the two situations, the last section, from 'Praise bounteous' (line 41) to the end, gives the conclusion – or rather two conclusions. Because love can appear in the most unlikely places, the poet tells the reader to 'Praise bounteous providence', or – what else? Find the word further on in the section that defines the other possible response. Both words are words of **command**.

<u>13</u> Like the description of the vultures in the first section, lines 43–47 ('even an ogre' to 'a cruel heart') describe a small moment of love in an ugly situation. Which words does the poet use to make the love seem small, and the rest of the situation seem ugly?

14 The last five lines, from 'or else despair' to the end, offer the opposite response. Why should 'despair' be a possible response? Is this an alternative response really, or a continuation of the thought? Think where the evil is 'lodged'.

Final thoughts

Read the poem again, following carefully the stages of the poet's thought as it unfolds. Do you think that the poet wants the reader to 'praise' or 'despair' in the end?

Comparisons

You might compare this poem with:

- Two Scavengers in a Truck . . . / Night of the Scorpion (people)
- Nothing's Changed / What Were They Like? (politics)
- This Room / Blessing (metaphor)
- Nothing's Changed / Two Scavengers in a Truck . . . (particular places)
- *from* Search For My Tongue / Island Man (two cultures)

Denise Levertov

a

Denise Levertov (1923–97) was one of the twentieth-century's foremost American poets. She was a long-term activist for peace and justice.

What Were They Like?

g

Glossary

Vietnam   The South-East Asian country of Vietnam was torn apart by a succession of wars from 1945 until the end of the Vietnamese War in 1975, when the American forces withdrew.

paddies   paddy fields are wet land where rice is grown

Read and revise

You can see from the page that the poem is organised into questions and answers. The poet clearly intends you to read all the questions first, and then all the answers. Read the poem through once, taking in the tone of all the questions read together, and the tone created by reading all the answers together.

1 How does the poet show that the first 9 lines are questions? Think about numbering, punctuation and sentence forms.

2 The replies in the rest of the poem are written in forms suitable for replies.

- Look at the beginnings of the responses to Questions 1 and 3, and Questions 2 and 4. Which repeated words are typical of replies?

- How is the beginning of Question 5 like another type of reply?

- The reply to Question 6 has a different feature. There is only one question in the second half of the poem, in the last line. Why do you think the poet has chosen to use this form here?

3 The questions are all in the past tense ('did', 'were', etc.). Why? What does this suggest about the Vietnamese culture?

4 These poems are entitled 'Different Cultures and Traditions'. Questions 1–6 are about the nature of the culture of Vietnam. What elements of culture (which could be about any culture) does the questioner ask about? There are the things they used (artefacts) – what else?

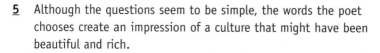
5 Although the questions seem to be simple, the words the poet chooses create an impression of a culture that might have been beautiful and rich.

- In Question 2, what does the word 'reverence' imply about the nature of the people? If they revered 'the opening of buds', what does this suggest about their nature? Think about what the opposite, killing buds, would imply.

- What does 'quiet laughter' (Question 3) imply about them? Think about both words.

- What is implied about their ornaments in Question 4? What does this say about what they might have valued?

- What does Question 5 imply about their culture?

- What does Question 6 imply about the nature of their voices? What does that say about them? Why do you think the poet includes this question? Think about the end of the poem.

6 The answers to the questions, read together, create a very different tone from the questions themselves. The following questions unpick some of the ideas in the answers – but which words can you find from the Answers 1–6 that create a tone of destruction and tragedy? You could begin with 'killed' in the second answer.

7 Look at Answer 1.

- How has the idea of 'lanterns of stone' in Question 1 been changed and used in the first line? Think what a lantern does.

- What does 'light hearts to stone' mean, do you think?

- Memory has obviously gone – but what else seems to have been destroyed with it? How does this add to the tone of this part of the poem?

8 The word 'once' in Answer 2 implies something in the past. What has been destroyed? What are the children compared to here, and why is it an apt comparison?

9 The answer to Question 3 is short. Why, do you think? Why is the laughter 'bitter'? Think of two reasons, based on two different meanings of 'bitter'.

10 In Answer 4, how does the poet make the idea of beauty seem distant? What has been destroyed? How has the poet altered and used the idea of 'bone' in Question 4 to add to the sense of destruction?

11 Look at the answer to Question 5.

- What has been destroyed?

- Why do you think the poet has included 'their life / was in rice and bamboo'? How does it add to the sense of destruction?

- What sort of life is pictured in the sentence beginning 'When peaceful clouds'?

- How does the poet create a sense of there being plenty of time in the sentence beginning 'When peaceful clouds'? Think about Question 5, which this is the answer to. How is the time taken to destroy this life shown to be short?

- What are the 'mirrors'? What does the word 'mirrors' imply about the fields before the bombs dropped?

12 Look at Answer 6.

- 'An echo' remains. What has been destroyed, then?

- What does 'the flight of moths in moonlight' suggest about their singing? How does the loss of this add to the sense of destruction?

- What is the answer to the question at the beginning of the last line? Think again why the poet chose this as the final question and answer. Notice the tense of the last line. Why is it 'silent now'?

Final thoughts

Read the poem through again, with the last sentence 'It is silent now' in mind. How does the whole poem lead up to this line? Think of as many ways as you can.

Comparisons

You might compare this poem with:
- Nothing's Changed / This Room (change)
- Nothing's Changed / Two Scavengers in a Truck . . . (politics)
- Limbo (unusual presentation)
- Presents from my Aunts . . . / Night of the Scorpion (specific cultural references)

Sujata Bhatt

a Sujata Bhatt was born in 1956 in Ahmedabad, India. She emigrated to the United States in 1968. As well as following a successful career as a poet, she has translated poems from Gujarati into English.

from Search For My Tongue

g **Glossary**

The script type which runs from line 17 to line 29 is Gujarati.
The words in brackets below each line of script form a transliteration into phonetic English sounds.

Mother tongue   your native or original language

Read and revise

This poem is about language, and the effect on language of living in a different place with people who speak a different language. 'Tongue' means two things – the language you speak, and the physical thing you use to speak it. Read the poem right through at least once, thinking about these two things.

1 The most striking thing about the appearance of the poem on the page is the use of two different languages, with the Gujarati script looking very different from the rest of the words.

- Notice where the Gujarati script is placed in the poem. How is it appropriate that this script is in the middle of the poem?

- The transliteration turns the Gujarati script into English sounds. In terms of 'tongues' which tongue is this? If you're not sure, how does this add to the message of the poem?

- Some readers, like the poet, will be familiar with both languages, but some will not. If you don't know the language, does it matter? Think what the poem is about, and how you might feel living with 'a foreign tongue' (line 7).

2 Lines 1–14 use 'I' and 'you', as though these were the words of a conversation between the speaker and another person translated into poetry.

- What has the speaker just said, before the 'conversation' is reported?

- How is a conversation a suitable form for the poet to choose for this poem?

41

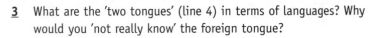

3 What are the 'two tongues' (line 4) in terms of languages? Why would you 'not really know' the foreign tongue?

4 How does the poet suggest very early in the poem that she is going to use the idea of another tongue, literally? Look at the way line 4 is expressed.

5 Why could you not 'use them both together' (line 8)? Think about both meanings of 'tongue'.

6 Lines 1–9 have imagined the idea of losing a tongue – but the sentence beginning at line 10 reminds the reader that this is a real situation for the speaker, and many other people. How does the poet use the idea of another physical tongue to make the situation seem unpleasant in lines 10–14? Think about the ideas suggested, and the words used. Notice which word is repeated, and where the word is placed on the line – how does this add to the effect?

7 Now look again at the last 8 lines of the poem, from line 31 to the end. The idea that the poet uses here is of the tongue being like a plant, which could grow again in the mouth.

- Find all the words that are about plants and growth in these lines.

- How does the poet convey the strength of the new growth of the mother tongue? Notice the word that is repeated four times, as well as other words and ideas.

- From lines 31 to 34, which different stages of plant growth are mentioned? How is it made clear that the growth is healthy?

- Why do you think the poet repeats the phrase 'the bud opens' in line 34? Think about the whole metaphor – is this a welcome growth, or not? A **metaphor** compares one thing to another directly, without using 'like' or 'as'.

- Does the last sentence from 'Everytime I think ...' imply that the speaker welcomes this return of the mother tongue? Think about the words used.

- 'Blossoms' is the natural outcome of the growth process. Again, does this suggest that this is welcome? What will the blossom actually result in?

Final thoughts

All of the last eight lines form an extended metaphor, comparing the tongue to the growth of a plant – a natural growth, that is. Why do you think the poet chose to do this? Read the whole poem again, with the ending in mind.

You might compare this poem with:

- Presents from my Aunts . . . / Hurricane Hits England (identity)
- Island Man / Half-Caste (people)
- Presents from my Aunts . . . / Half-Caste (first person)
- *from* Unrelated Incidents / Limbo (unusual presentation)
- Night of the Scorpion / Hurricane Hits England (cultural references)
- This Room / Blessing (metaphor)
- Presents from my Aunts . . . / Hurricane Hits England (two cultures)

Comparisons

Sujata Bhatt *from* Search For My Tongue

Tom Leonard

a Tom Leonard, who was born in 1944 in Glasgow, writes poetry which is rooted in local language and working class culture. His writing is often political because, as he says, 'language itself in Britain is a political issue'.

from Unrelated Incidents

g ### Glossary

The words of the poem are a phonetic representation of words spoken in a Glaswegian accent – so 'and' becomes 'n' (line 4), for instance. It would help you to 'hear' every word either by listening to a tape of somebody reading the poem in a Glaswegian accent, or better still by listening to somebody from Glasgow reading it. However, it's not absolutely necessary – you should be able to work most of it out. And, anyway, the language itself is part of the point of the poem.

Read and revise

The best way to get to grips with this poem is to read it aloud – several times, till you start to get the sense of it. The language is an approximation of spoken language written down, after all.

1 The layout of the poem is unusual, because of what it is representing. The shape is like an autocue – a device used by newsreaders (and others) that allows them to read while still looking at the audience. How does this explain the number of words in the lines?

2 Now look at the punctuation. What is missing which you might expect in written English? What is still there, and why?

3 There's another feature of written English that isn't here, as the language is read, then spoken. Look at line 15, for instance. What should be here, in written standard English?

4 Who is 'thi man' (lines 3–4)? Why does he talk with a BBC accent, not a regional accent?

5 Who are 'yoo scruff', that the man addresses his words to, do you think? Where do they live? What do they do?

6 Truth ('trooth'), and how it is perceived, is at the heart of this poem. Why doesn't the man think that 'yoo scruff' would believe the truth, if it was told to them in their own words, do you think? What does this reveal about his attitude to them, as well as their attitude to him?

7 'Jist wonna you scruff tokn' (lines 22–23). What does this suggest about the man's attitude to working class language – and to 'yoo scruff' themselves?

8 'Thirza right way ti spell ana right way ti tok it' (lines 24–27). Does the poet think that there is a 'right way' of spelling and talking, do you think? Think about the language that the poem is actually written in.

9 The man talks in 'yir right way a spellin' in the poem, but says that 'this is ma trooth'. Who does the truth belong to, according to him? What is the poet saying about class attitudes here?

10 'Yooz doant no thi trooth yirsellz' continues the same attitude, but the reason is that 'yi canny talk right'. What does this suggest about the connection between language, truth, class and power? Who has the power?

11 What is the message of the last two words, 'belt up'? What are 'yoo scruff ' being denied altogether?

Final thoughts

Read the poem again, thinking about the voice of the speaker. How does the poet gain power for his message by 'speaking' the words in a Glaswegian accent?

Comparisons

You might compare this poem with:

- Nothing's Changed / *from* Search For My Tongue (identity)
- Nothing's Changed / Two Scavengers in a Truck . . . (politics – class)
- *from* Search For My Tongue / Limbo (unusual presentation)
- Limbo / Half-Caste (non-standard English)
- Half-Caste / Presents from my Aunts . . . (two cultures)

John Agard

a | John Agard came to England from Guyana in 1977. He is of mixed race himself – his Portuguese mother is from Guyana, but his father is black.

Half-Caste

g |
Glossary

caste	an old word meaning the racial group someone was born into
half-caste	meant someone of mixed race, but implied rejection, and is now seen as an insulting term
Picasso	a famous twentieth-century artist

Read and revise

Read the poem through once, enjoying the repetitions and the voice. The poem reads best if read aloud – it's written that way.

1 The language of the poem is a mixture of standard and non-standard English. The phonetic spelling captures Caribbean pronunciation, and some of the grammar reflects Caribbean patois.

- Find examples of both of these in 'so spiteful dem don't want de sun pass' (line 21). Find an example of a standard English line.

- Why do you think the poet writes in a mixture of these two language forms? Think about the effect on the reader – and what the poem is about.

2 The punctuation of the poem is certainly non-standard. What punctuation is 'missing', and what punctuation can you find in its place? Why do you think the poet has made this choice? Remember that the poem is meant to be spoken aloud, and think about the effect a full stop can have on the voice.

3 There are very few capital letters in the poem. Find them, and try to decide why the poet has used them in these places.

4 Is this poem set in a particular culture? Think about place, attitudes, and language. Be careful, though – what culture do Picasso and Tchaikovsky belong to? Perhaps the poet is challenging some assumptions about language and culture.

5 The poem is divided into four sections. Decide why the divisions have been placed where they are, by working out what each section is about. Is the second section about the person the poem is addressed to, or the idea that the person has expressed? Ask the same question about the third section.

6 Much of the structure of the poem is built around repetitions, and sentence forms.

- Find each repetition of the phrase 'Explain yuself'. How are two of the uses apt introductions to sections of the poem?

- Some of these sentences are commands, some are statements, and some are questions. Look at the divisions set by the gaps between sections, and by the forward slashes. Which parts are commands, which are statements, and which are questions? Do the last three lines of the poem form a command or a statement?

7 What is the tone of the first section (lines 1–3), do you think? How is the poet using humour to make a point?

8 There are four divisions in the second section (lines 4–30), marked by the forward slashes. Look at the three that begin 'Explain yuself'. Work out the structure within each of these divisions – what else is repeated? The word 'mix', which is part of this structure, occurs at the beginning of the line each time. Why do you think the poet repeats this word, and why does he place it here?

9 The questions in this section make fun of the idea that mixing colours is unnatural, or wrong. How are the Picasso and Tchaikovsky ideas silly? Why do you think the poet chooses to end this section with the Tchaikovsky rather than the Picasso?

10 Look at the lines about weather (lines 10–22).

- How are colours mixed here?

- Why has the poet chosen the word 'overcast' (line 20) to describe a dark sky, do you think? Remember the title of the poem. Look at lines 45 and 46 for another playful use of words.

11 Lines 33–34 and 35–36 form another repetition of sentence structure. 'Ear' and 'eye' emerge again later in the section. Why is the speaker using the 'keen' half of each? Think about who the person is that is being listened to and looked at, and what they have said.

12 Using 'half-a-hand' (line 39) is another humorous idea, making fun of the idea of half a person. It's not just humorous, though – the poet is very serious about this, after all. Think what shaking hands with somebody means. Why might the speaker only want to offer 'half-a-hand' to this person?

13 The idea of somebody casting 'half-a-shadow' by moonlight is the stuff of horror stories. Whose fears might the poet be mocking by introducing this idea?

14 Time first appears in the section at line 37, 'when I'm introduced to yu'. Where else is time mentioned in the section? How does line 47 introduce a different time? Why must it be different?

15 Look at the last three lines of the second section (lines 48–50).

- This repeated structure emphasises a change in the poem's language. Which word is new?

- 'Eye' and 'ear' are repeated from earlier, but now clearly mean how somebody perceives something. Has the person been looking and listening properly so far? 'Mind' is added, too. What has the person being addressed not been doing so far?

16 Look at the last three lines of the poem, which form the final section, and change the feeling and tone of the poem.

- There are many repeated words and structures in the last eight lines of the third section. Find as many as you can, and then look at these last three lines of the poem. What repetitions are there here? Why do you think the poet creates this change?

- Through most of the poem, the speaker demands answers. How is this different?

- What conditions does the speaker set for telling the other half of his story? What will 'yu' have to do, to hear and understand the speaker completely?

Final thoughts

Read the poem again. Much of the poem is at least half-joking, and much is like a song. How does this change at the end?

You might compare this poem with:

- Presents from my Aunts . . . / Hurricane Hits England (people)
- Nothing's Changed / *from* Search For My Tongue (first person)
- Limbo / *from* Unrelated Incidents (non-standard English)
- Hurricane Hits England / Vultures (universal idea)
- Presents from my Aunts . . . / *from* Unrelated Incidents (two cultures)

Comparisons

Derek Walcott

Derek Walcott was born in St Lucia in 1930. In 1992 he was awarded the Nobel Prize for Literature for his poetry 'sustained by a historical vision, the outcome of a multicultural commitment'.

a

Love After Love

Read and revise

This is an intriguing poem – how can you greet yourself? Read the poem through once, noticing that 'your self' is printed as two words in line 7.

1 Actions belonging to ceremonies are used several times in this poem – suggesting that this is an important moment, perhaps, one to be marked by ceremony.

- Pick out the words that belong to the ceremony of welcoming somebody to your house. Some words are repeated, to add to the effect.

- There's a reference to religious ceremony here too. Find it in the second stanza.

2 The idea of something that is repeated, but different, occurs first in the title. How?

3 Look at the first stanza (lines 1–5).

- Apart from 'your', which word is used three times in this stanza? What does it suggest about the future? Remember that the poem might be read as a message to the reader.

- Which words in the stanza suggest that when this thing happens, it will be a happy event?

- Why do you think that the idea of looking 'in your own mirror' (line 4) is useful in this poem? Think about line 5. How does it help to make solid the idea of two selves?

4 Line 7 is a key line for understanding the poem.

- This stranger is somebody who was 'your self'. You, in other words, but in the past. Before what happened, do you think? Think about the title.

- This old 'self' has become a 'stranger'. Which of the selves is the true 'self', do you think? Notice the effect of making 'your self' two words.

- What will 'you' learn to do when this old 'self', who has become a stranger, arrives? Why has the poet included the word 'again' after 'love', do you think?

5 The giving of wine and bread, referred to in line 8, might make the reader think of a religious ceremony, as well as the welcoming of a stranger. Which ceremony is this, and what do the wine and bread represent? (You might have to research this.) You might then connect these things with the 'heart' in the same line. How do all these things amount to a whole 'giving'?

6 Who is 'the stranger who has loved you / all your life'? (lines 9–10). The phrase 'loved you / all your life' is broken by a change in stanza, not just a new line. The pause created makes the reader notice a particular phrase. Which one? Why this one, do you think?

7 'Whom you ignored / for another' (lines 10–11) has the same effect, lifting out 'for another'. Who is this? It might be the other 'self' who replaced the original one – who else might it be? Think about the following two lines.

8 How does the 'stranger' know you 'by heart'? This is the second time 'heart' has been used – see line 8. 'Heart' has a number of meanings, and 'by heart' adds to the list. Looking at the two appearances of 'heart' here, which meanings are referred to? How does the use of the word 'heart' help to suggest which the true 'self' is?

9 Look at the sentence beginning 'Take down the love letters' (line 12).

- What things in these lines suggest a love affair, that is now over? Think about the title again.

- If 'your own images' are peeled from the mirror, what is revealed underneath?

- What do you think 'your own images' means here? Does 'image' suggest something false?

10 The last line of the poem returns to the idea of welcoming. 'Eat' (line 6) has become 'Feast'. What is the difference, and what does it suggest about 'your life'? The previous few lines have been about the past – what does this suggest about the future?

Final thoughts

Read the poem again, thinking about the title and line 5.

Comparisons

You might compare this poem with:
- This Room / *from* Search For My Tongue (identity)
- Vultures / Nothing's Changed (universal idea)
- Hurricane Hits England (affirmation of life)
- This Room (domestic life / metaphor)

Derek Walcott Love After Love

Imtiaz Dharker

a ⎯ Imtiaz Dharker lives in Bombay in India.

This Room

Read and revise

Read the poem through once, looking for the key sentence as you do – it's not at the beginning!

1 This poem is a thought, really, about some moments in life that are special – but lots of very definite things are mentioned, including feet and hands. Which sentence doesn't have any definite things in it, only ideas?

2 Which sentence is specifically about life?

3 Counting the number of lines, which sentence is exactly in the middle of the poem, so that it refers to what has gone before and sets the idea for what comes after?

4 Look at the sentence beginning 'This is the time and place' (line 10).

   • A lot of events are described in the poem. Lines 10 and 11 are not an event – what are they? The language of the rest of the poem is very dramatic. What sort of language is this?

   • How does the punctuation at the end of line 11 increase the sense of something definite being said?

   • The poet mentions a lot of the 'daily furniture of our lives' in the poem. What examples can you find of the things around us every day, from the whole poem? Don't stop at any fewer than seven things.

   • How has the poet illustrated the idea of 'the improbable' in the poem? You should find lots of examples!

5 Look at the first stanza (lines 1–5).

   • What is described here which is physically impossible, not just 'improbable'?

   • A room can't literally be 'in search of' anything, because it isn't a living thing. When an object is described as though it

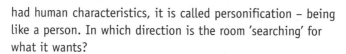

had human characteristics, it is called personification – being like a person. In which direction is the room 'searching' for what it wants?

- Which words does the poet use in these lines to suggest that freedom is being sought?

6 Look at the second stanza, from 'The bed is lifting' to the end of line 9.

- In which direction are things moving? Which words tell you?
- Which word here is another personification – something things can't have?
- There's a movement upwards throughout the poem, but there's also a movement from dark to light. Which words or ideas here suggest moving from darkness to light? Why do you think the poet wanted to use this idea?

7 Look at lines 14–18, from 'Pots and pans' to 'the door'.

- There's some more personification here. What can't pots and pans actually do? Which word suggests a collection of people rather than things?
- Where is movement upwards suggested again?
- Lots of different parts of the room have been mentioned, but 'No one is looking for the door'. What does this usually mean? Why has the poet used exactly these words here to convey what she means?

8 Look at the last four lines of the poem, from 'In all this excitement' (line 19) to the end.

- Most of the poem has described the behaviour of inanimate objects. The first person 'I' appears for the first time at line 20. Whose 'excitement' has the poem been about, do you think?
- If the speaker is wondering about where she has left her feet, what does this suggest she is doing? Think about the movement mentioned before in the poem.
- Being 'outside' suggests standing back, or looking on. The speaker's hands are 'clapping' looking at what is happening. Why, do you think? Think of two reasons for hands to be clapping.

Final thoughts

The poem could be about the excitement of moments when things change – 'when the improbable happens'. At moments like these, all our surroundings seem to share our excitement – or it's just as if they do. Read the poem right through again with this in mind, noticing the effect of placing the key sentence in the middle, and identifying the person at the end.

Comparisons

You might compare this poem with:

• Love After Love / *from* Search For My Tongue (identity)
• Nothing's Changed / What Were They Like? (change)
• Nothing's Changed / Night of the Scorpion (first person)
• *from* Search For My Tongue / Half-Caste (metaphor)
• Love After Love / Hurricane Hits England (universal idea)

Niyi Osundare

a | Niyi Osundare is a contemporary Nigerian poet.

Not my Business

Read and revise

This is a simple poem, with a powerful ending. Read it through once. When you get to the end, how do you know what is going to happen?

1 The form of the poem is a verse followed by a refrain – repeated lines, like a chorus. The fourth verse, however, has no refrain. Why has the poet not finished with the refrain, do you think?

2 There's another pattern in the structure of the poem. Look at the first line of each verse – what is mentioned in each one?

3 The language of the first two verses is violent. Find the words suggesting violence – you should find at least four. There is no violence in the last verse, though. Why not, do you think?

4 The language of the poem is standard English – almost. Look at the second line of the refrain. How is this non-standard English?

5 Look at the first verse (lines 1–4).

- Why do you think the poet uses the simile 'soft like clay' (line 2)? A **simile** is the word for one thing being compared to another, using 'like' or 'as'. What does this simile make you imagine about the beating of Akanni?

- Why do you think the interior of the jeep is described as 'the belly'? Think about the verb at the beginning of line 3. A metaphor is the word for one thing being compared to another directly, without using 'like' or 'as'.

6 In the second verse (lines 8–11), find the two violent words again – both verbs. Notice where they come in the line, and look back at the first verse. What do you notice? Why do you think the poet has put these words where they are?

7 There is no violence in the third verse (lines 15–18), but there is injustice. What is the injustice? Which line indicates there is injustice? Why does the poet mention that Chinwe's record is 'stainless'?

Niyi Osundare Not my Business

55

8 Now look at the last verse (lines 22–26).

- The knock on the door comes when the yam is being held in the 'hungry hand'. Why do you think the poet has made this choice? The refrain suggests that the speaker is safe – is he? What is going to happen, do you think?

- Lawns aren't usually 'bewildered'. Who is 'bewildered', do you think?

- How does the poet create a sense of threat in the last line? Think about the repeated word, and the effect of the last word.

Final thoughts

Read the poem again, thinking about the title and the refrain this time. What does 'not my business' seem to mean when you read the refrain after each of the first three verses? How does the title become ironic after you've read the last verse?

Comparisons

You might compare this poem with:

- Island Man / Nothing's Changed (people)
- Nothing's Changed / Two Scavengers in a Truck . . . (specific cultural references)
- *from* Unrelated Incidents / Half-Caste (use of repetition)

Moniza Alvi

> Moniza Alvi was born in Pakistan in 1954, but has spent most of her life living and working in England.

Presents from my Aunts in Pakistan

> **Glossary**
>
> | | |
> |---|---|
> | **salwar kameez** | a long, flowing tunic style dress and trousers worn in Pakistan |
> | **filigree** | a lacy ornamental work of fine gold wire |
> | **mirror work** | tiny sequins used as decoration on clothes |
> | **Shalimar Gardens** | a green and peaceful walled retreat in Lahore |

Read and revise

This is a poem about two cultures – the one the speaker lives in now, and the one she left behind as a child. Read the poem through once, noticing how there are many references to both cultures.

1 Read the poem again, picking out all the references to things that come from Pakistan. Then read again, picking out all the things that are associated more with life in the West.

2 There are eight sections in the poem. Make sure you can see the divisions between them, and then notice that in every section both cultures are mentioned. Why do you think the poet has chosen to do this, rather than writing sections about each? Think about what the poem is about, and the speaker's own position in the cultures.

3 The first section is richly descriptive. The poet uses these descriptive elements:

- colours
- shapes
- comparisons with fruit.

How many examples can you find of each of these?

4 Most of this section is about the presents from Pakistan, but even here the poet reminds you that the speaker now lives in England. Where?

5 'Snapped, drew blood' (line 9) suggests what about the bangles? Think about the life the speaker lives in England. Can both these cultures work for the speaker? What does the incident with the bangles suggest?

Moniza Alvi Presents from my Aunts in Pakistan

<u>6</u> Look at the second section (lines 16–26).

- Why does the speaker feel 'alien in the sitting-room' (line 17)? Why do you think the speaker feels 'alien'? Alien to which culture? Why does the poet choose the 'sitting-room'?

- What does the longing for 'denim and corduroy' suggest?

- Why do you think the speaker is 'aflame' in the costume? Think about colour, and how she is feeling.

- Rising up 'out of its fire' suggests the legend of the phoenix, a mythical bird that was reborn from its own funeral pyre. What couldn't the speaker do, though?

<u>7</u> The next section (lines 27–33) is about the lamp, but reflects the poem's concerns.

- The lamp is made from camel-skin. Which culture does this reflect?

- The speaker admires the clothes which represent the culture of her aunts, but doesn't feel that she belongs to them – 'I could never be as lovely / as those clothes'. How does a similar attitude appear in these lines?

- The lines mention a 'transformation'. How does this word reflect one of the concerns of the poem?

<u>8</u> The next section (lines 34–39) is short, but is full of reminders of both cultures which overlap here.

- In the first sentence, how is a reminder of one culture affected by a reminder of another?

- Each of the second and third sentences contains elements of both cultures. What are they? They also contrast with each other, though. What is ironic about the aunts' request for cardigans?

<u>9</u> In the next section (lines 40–54), remind yourself of the elements of both cultures that are present.

- The mirrors sewn into the salwar kameez are important in the rest of the poem, as the speaker tries to 'glimpse' herself. Which two pictures from her story are mentioned in the rest of the section?

- The speaker 'tried to glimpse myself' (line 45). Why would she want to see herself? Think what the whole poem is about, and what the speaker's problem is.

- At the end of the section, the speaker remembers that she 'found myself alone / playing with a tin boat'. The real boat has shipped her from one culture to another. Why might she be 'alone'? Think about her situation then, and in the whole poem.

10 The next section (lines 55–64) continues the pictures in the mirrors.

- There are three pictures presented here. What are they?

- 'Conflict, a fractured land' refers to war in the speaker's country of birth – but how does it also remind you of the speaker herself, and how she feels?

- The final picture here, of the aunts, begins to feel like the ending of the poem – why? Think about the way the poet has structured the poem.

11 The final section (lines 65–69) presents the last picture that the speaker sees in a mirror.

- This must be one of the speaker's earliest memories, yet she still feels 'of no fixed nationality'. Why, do you think? Remember this is an older girl looking back.

- Why do you think the speaker uses the phrase 'of no fixed nationality' so near to the end of the poem, and at the end of a line aligned to the right? Think of the effect on the reader, who has read the whole poem now.

- Why has the poet chosen this as the last picture of the poem? Think where the speaker must be as she stares at the Shalimar Gardens – not just the country, but her physical position.

Final thoughts

As you have seen, this poem is about the effect of changing cultures on an individual. Read the poem again, concentrating on the speaker's feelings. Which are the key phrases in the poem that state what her problem is?

Comparisons

You might compare this poem with:

- *from* Search For My Tongue / Hurricane Hits England (identity)
- Nothing's Changed / *from* Search For My Tongue (change)
- Nothing's Changed / Half-Caste (first person)
- Nothing's Changed / Blessing (description)
- Hurricane Hits England / What Were They Like? (cultural references)
- *from* Search For My Tongue / Island Man (two cultures)
- Night of the Scorpion / What Were They Like? (traditions)

Grace Nichols

a Grace Nichols was born and educated in Guyana in the West Indies. She came to Britain in 1977.

Hurricane Hits England

g

Glossary	
hurricane	hurricane-force storms hit the South of England in October 1987, felling 15 million trees
Shango	the mythical African Lord of war and fertility, and also the god of thunder
Oya	the wife of Shango, known for her intelligence and independence, but also the strong wind which precedes the thunder
Hattie	the name of the hurricane which devastated the Caribbean in October 1961

Read and revise

This poem is about a woman who moves from one culture to another, and feels isolated from it, until a natural event brings her to a new understanding. Read the poem through once, noticing the cultural references and the movement from questions to a definite conclusion.

1 The poem is structured around different sentence forms – **statements**, **commands** and **questions**. Look at all the sentences in the poem, identifying them as statement, command or question. Identify exactly where the questions begin. In what ways might the statements at the end be the answer to the questions? You might come back to this at the end.

2 The poem is arranged in stanzas of irregular length. The sentence forms partly explain the arrangement. Only one stanza consists of a single line, which makes it stand out from the rest of the poem. Why do you think the poet has made this choice? Think about the question itself, and notice where it comes in the changes from one sentence form to another.

3 Certain words are repeated. There are three groups of three in the language of the poem. Looking at the beginning of the lines will give you two of them. Where is the third? How does this fit the conclusion of the poem? 'Conclusion' has two meanings, remember.

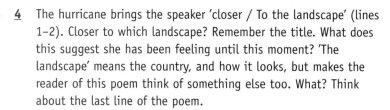

4 The hurricane brings the speaker 'closer / To the landscape' (lines 1–2). Closer to which landscape? Remember the title. What does this suggest she has been feeling until this moment? 'The landscape' means the country, and how it looks, but makes the reader of this poem think of something else too. What? Think about the last line of the poem.

5 The wind is described as a 'howling ship' (line 4). The sea is mentioned several times in this poem, perhaps not surprisingly. A ship, however, suggests a voyage. How does this remind you of the situation of the speaker?

6 Which words in lines 4–7 convey the strength and threat of the hurricane?

7 Some of the words are doing something else, though. What does the word 'ancestral' imply? Whose past is being summoned up, like a 'spectre' (a ghost)? How might the wind be 'reassuring'? What does it remind the speaker of?

8 Line 8 is the first change of sentence form, from statement to command – 'Talk to me'. There's another change, though. How does the word 'me' mark a change from the first stanza? Why do you think the poet has chosen to begin in third person, and move to first? Think about the feelings of being distanced, and being involved.

9 The names of the gods recall the culture that the speaker used to belong to, and the name of the hurricane recalls an event in that place. How else does the poet remind you of the old place in the second stanza – and how close she feels to it?

10 Lines 13 and 14 form the beginning of the questions that the speaker asks – this is what she wants the gods to 'talk' to her about. 'Tell me' is the stem for all the questions, which run to line 27. These lines are the transition, though. Is this sentence a command, or a question?

11 The hurricane is compared to 'old tongues' (line 16). How is the hurricane a reminder of 'old tongues'? Think about her past, and the second stanza.

12 What 'old tongues' are referred to in the poem, and what 'new places' (lines 16–18)?

13 The fourth stanza (lines 19–22) describes lightning – but the speaker is asking about its meaning. Changing from light to dark quickly might remind you of where the speaker actually is. How? Look back to the first stanza. But 'illumination' can mean something else, too, in the same way that 'darkness' can mean ignorance. What 'illumination' does the speaker have at the end of the poem?

14 How does the poet remind you of the sea again in the fifth stanza (lines 23–26)?

15 Line 27 is the only single line stanza, and it is the last question – the culmination of the questioning, before the answers. What do you think the speaker's heart is 'unchained' from? What was it 'chained' to? Is this a good thing, or not? Think carefully about this – there are several possible meanings.

16 The answer to the questions seems to be to change. How do the verbs in lines 29–31 suggest movement and change? The speaker's resolve seems to be to follow nature – how?

17 A 'mystery' (line 32) is something difficult to understand, but magical too. What has 'come to' the speaker has been hard to understand, but it is magical. What is it, apart from the hurricane coming to England? Think about the last line.

18 How does the speaker compare herself to nature in lines 33 and 34? Why? Think about the first two lines. Why does she feel she has been a 'frozen' lake? Think about how she has felt in England up till this moment. The wind is from the tropics – 'Tropical Oya of the Weather' (line 28).

Final thoughts

The hurricane from the tropics lets her know that 'the earth is the earth is the earth' (line 36). The poem has mentioned old places and new places; old tongues; the past and the present; old homes and new homes and how somebody moving from one place to another feels. What does the last line of the poem say about all of this? How does the poet underline the importance of this, by the way the last line is written?

Comparisons

You might compare this poem with:

- Love After Love / Presents from my Aunts . . . (identity)
- Island Man / Half-Caste (people)
- Nothing's Changed / Presents from my Aunts . . . (first person)
- Night of the Scorpion / *from* Search For My Tongue (cultural references)
- Presents from my Aunts . . . (places)
- Two Scavengers in a Truck / Half-Caste (universal ideas)
- Presents from my Aunts . . . / Island Man (two cultures)
- Limbo / What Were They Like? (traditions)

? Questions

Foundation Tier

Compare the ways in which the poets present people in **Night of the Scorpion** and **one** other poem of your choice from this selection.

Write about:

- what the different people are like
- what the poets think about them
- how the language brings out what the people are like
- how the language shows what the poets think about the people
- which poem you prefer and why.

Higher Tier

Compare **Hurricane Hits England** with **one** other poem, showing how poets reveal their ideas and feelings about the particular cultures they are writing about.

Comparing poems from Different Cultures and Traditions

The examination questions on the poems from Different Cultures and Traditions in the *Anthology* will ask you to write about two poems, and compare them. When you're thinking about the individual poems in the clusters, and especially when you're revising them before the exam, it's a good idea to think about them together. That's why the questions on individual poems are followed by suggestions for other poems to compare with them.

The section here shows some thoughts about comparing two poems, though of course you might be asked about any of them. The suggestions are presented in note form – the sort of notes you might make about them when you're thinking about comparing. You would need to add plenty of evidence from the text for a full answer.

The simplest way to think about similarities and differences between the poems is to think through each of the Assessment Objectives that are tested. So, the notes are arranged in these sections:

*   meanings / interpretations
*   linguistic / structural / presentational devices
*   language variations
*   cultures.

The two poems being compared here are **Night of the Scorpion** and **Two Scavengers in a Truck, Two Beautiful People in a Mercedes.**

	Night of the Scorpion	Two Scavengers in a Truck . . .
Meanings / interpretations		
Story	Dramatic story – events, resolution	No story, only a momentary juxtaposition
People	Peasants / mother ('only said') father / watcher	Truck people / Mercedes people
Class	'peasants' v 'sceptic, rationalist'	'scavengers', 'garbagemen' v architect's office confirmed by dress and appearance –'grungy' v 'cool' and various details

continued

Emotion	Many feelings – of peasants / father / mother / watcher	No feelings – emotionless, a still picture
Attitudes	Attitudes of mother / father clear	Not so clear though writer's attitude implied via 'gulf ... of democracy'

Linguistic / structural / presentational devices

Structure	A story, chronologically structured, remembered	No narrative – a moment, structured as scene setting / details about people / reflection. Present tense
Language	Written in whole sentences – one continuous piece, bar break before last three lines	No main verbs / full stops words add details. Four stanzas, reflecting structure as above
Presentation	Lines justified left (conventional)	Left, right and centred – more jagged to read, less continuous – allows for building of a thought in unusual way

Language variations

	Language reflects culture of religion – 'Evil One' and string of 'May ...' reflecting prayer and evil v good	'hip', 'cool', 'grungy' reflects American modern culture

Place and culture

	Rain / scorpion / rice / peasants / holy man	Garbagemen / Mercedes / plastic blazers / short skirt / sunglasses

Structuring a response to poems from Different Cultures and Traditions

When you set about responding to a question in the examination, it's important to take some time to plan your work. In this section there's an example of a plan for a particular question – but remember that there will be a number of other ways to plan a successful answer. There will be two questions to choose from in the exam paper, each of which will name a poem. Suppose that the question you choose in the exam is this:

Compare the ways in which the poets present people in **Night of the Scorpion** and **one** other poem of your choice from this selection.

Write about:

- what the different people are like
- what the poets think about them
- how the language brings out what the people are like
- how the language shows what the poets think about the people
- which poem you prefer and why.

You could choose almost any of the other poems to answer this question. If, for example, you decided to use the same two poems as in 'Comparing poems' – adding **Two Scavengers in a Truck . . .** to **Night of the Scorpion** – how would you go about it? A table has been provided to help you to think along the right lines.

One way of structuring a response is simply to follow the points one by one, if these are offered – but you don't have to do it this way. However, you do have to cover what they suggest at some point in your writing, so it's important to look carefully at what they are asking. Looking at the sections in this question, it's clear that the first one is asking something about meaning and interpretation, and the second one about language. The final section asks for your opinion, so you mustn't forget this – the examiner wants to know what you think. This might offer you the chance to say things which you haven't already said, especially material which relates to the Assessment Objectives. The plan, with a little detail to indicate what you're going to write about in each section, might look something like this:

Night of the Scorpion	Two Scavengers in a Truck . . .
1 Different people / what the poets think about them	
Peasants religious / father desperate, loves mother / mother grateful, loves children. Effect on watcher? Poet's view not given, but if watcher, clearly affected by mother's unselfishness, and father – perhaps reason for memory, and writing of poem.	Descriptions only – gives details to show differences – perhaps favours garbagemen – words applied to cool couple, and final verse suggesting egalitarian agenda.
2 Language showing people / poet's attitude	
Religious language shows peasants / 'every', 'even' shows father / 'only' showing mother. Perhaps break before last three lines shows impression on watching child – therefore poet? Watcher's horror shown by details and 'I watched' repetition.	'red plastic', 'grungy', 'gargoyle', 'scavengers' v 'hip', 'cool', 'elegant' etc. Poet's attitude by 'small gulf / in high seas / of this democracy'.

3 Your preference (You need to honestly answer which! However, you could mention here some of the comparative elements you haven't mentioned, because you've been busy – rightly – answering the question. So, you could prefer one over the other because:)

Night of the Scorpion has a clear, affecting narrative, told in a chronological sequence. **Night of the Scorpion**, isn't as appealing as **Two Scavengers in a Truck . . .** because it doesn't have a political message.	**Two Scavengers in a Truck . . .** is rather lacking in emotions, there isn't really a narrative, and the lines are arranged untidily. **Two Scavengers in a Truck . . .** has a political message which adds more meaning to the story the poet has told.

This is a pretty detailed plan, but when you go into the exam you should know the poems so well that you could write a plan like this without having to open your *Anthology* at all. You should probably only have to refer to it to look at some details. You might well think of a lot more to say as you write, which is fine, but if you stick to the outlines of your plan it will help you to answer the question effectively. Remember – you must give evidence from the texts to back up the points and comments that you make.

Section 2
English Literature

How the English Literature Anthology fits into the course

The AQA A English Literature course is assessed through a terminal examination, which counts for 70 per cent, and coursework, which counts for 30 per cent, of the final mark.

In the examination, there are two sections, A and B. Section A has questions on Pre-1914 prose, and is worth 30 per cent of the total marks. Section B has questions on Pre-1914 and Post-1914 poetry, based on the poems in the *Anthology*, and is worth 40 per cent of the total mark.

The *Anthology* short stories selection is one of the choices in Section A – you will have chosen to do these or a novel from the AQA A list. If you are doing the short stories, you have a choice of one of three questions.

Section B, on Pre-1914 and Post-1914 poetry, is more complicated. You have to choose to study two of the four poets in the Anthology, **either** Seamus Heaney and Gillian Clarke **or** Carol Ann Duffy and Simon Armitage. In the examination, you are offered a choice of three questions on each pair of poets. Each question will ask you to compare **four** poems – **one** by each of your chosen pair, and **two** from the Pre-1914 Poetry Bank. Each question will name at least one poem, and you have to choose which other poems to write about in response to the question.

What the examiners are looking for

The Assessment Objectives

The Assessment Objectives for any examination syllabus show what candidates have to do in their examinations for that syllabus. Examiners have to decide how well individual candidates have fulfilled these objectives in their examination performance, and give marks accordingly. Here are the Assessment Objectives for GCSE English Literature. Candidates must demonstrate their ability to:

- **Respond to texts critically, sensitively and in detail, selecting suitable ways to convey their response, using textual evidence as appropriate.**
  This simply means that you have to show that you can think about your texts, not just repeat what they say, and that you should be able to support what you have to say about the texts with some evidence, through quotations or other means of showing your knowledge. The more sensitive, detailed and organised you can be in your response, the better.

- **Explore how language, structure and forms contribute to the meanings of texts, considering different approaches to texts and alternative interpretations.**
  This emphasises that you should be able to write not just about what a text means, but how it is written; about writers' methods and devices, and the ways in which a writer's style can support and add to what he or she has to say. Also, you should be able to think about the same words or texts having a range of possible meanings, rather than just one.

- **Explore relationships and comparisons within and between texts, selecting and evaluating relevant material.**
  Comparison – how we understand one thing through comparing it to another – is at the heart of literature in all sorts of ways. Working out 'comparisons within texts' has much to do with writers' devices, and so is connected to the second Assessment Objective above. The questions on the *Anthology* in the examination will ask you to make 'comparisons between texts' – to compare one short story with another, or several poems with each other, in what they say and how they say it. To do this, you have to choose the right material to look at and assess. In the Pre-1914 and Post-1914 poetry questions, you will have a significant choice to make, in that you will have to choose which poems to compare with the named poem or poems. You will need to choose poems that you can compare effectively in response to the question you choose.

What the examiners will expect to see

The questions on the examination paper will be designed to test how well the candidates can fulfil the Assessment Objectives through writing about their chosen texts in response to the questions. So what will examiners expect to see?

Simply, they will want to see that you know your texts, and can think about them. *Knowing your texts* means not only being familiar with the details, but also understanding what they mean (in your view) and how they're written, and being able to move around them confidently to support what you have to say, without necessarily having to look them up all the time! Of course, you also have to compare the poems that you are writing about, and the examiners would look to see if you had managed to do this right through your response.

Thinking about your texts means showing your opinions and understanding of the texts in response to the questions that you have been asked. This may seem very obvious – but often candidates try to write down everything they know about a text, rather than answering the question, hoping that some of it will be relevant. This isn't the right way to go about it, just as telling the story isn't the right way to go about it. That's why learning an 'answer' before you go into the exam is never the right thing to do – after all, you don't know what the question will be! Go into the exam knowing your texts, and respond directly to the questions.

Poetry

Seamus Heaney

a Seamus Heaney is an Irish poet, born in 1939 in County Derry. In 1995 he was awarded the Nobel Prize for Literature.

Storm on the Island

g
Glossary

wizened	dried up
stooks	groups of sheaves of grain
strafes	rake with gun fire at close range, especially from the air
salvo	a number of guns firing at once

Read and revise

Read the poem through twice – the first time to get a sense of what the poem is about, and the second time focusing on the shift from a feeling of safety to a feeling of fear.

1 The first two lines establish a sense of readiness and strength. The poet uses a number of techniques to do this, which gives you a good opportunity to show that you can analyse how a poet produces effects.

- How are the first three words strong? Think about the length of the statement, and how the poet makes you stop after the first three words. Compare the feeling this suggests with the first word of the last line of the poem.

- Pick out the words in the first two lines that suggest strength and solidity – a number of these together reinforce the feeling.

- The rhythm of these lines is very regular and strong. When you say the second line aloud, how many beats are there in the line? Which words do the stresses fall on? You won't be able to do this as easily with any of the later lines – try it. The poet uses a number of devices later to break the rhythm up, and with it the sense of solidity.

- How many syllables do the words in the second line have? Again, compare this with any of the lines past line 5. This is an end-stopped line – there is a full stop at the end. How does that add to what the poet is doing here?

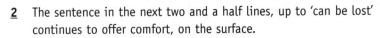

English Literature: Poetry

2 The sentence in the next two and a half lines, up to 'can be lost' continues to offer comfort, on the surface.

- What can't be lost?`

- Rhyme joins things together – makes them solid, if you like. Which two words here are joined by sounding almost the same? Now look back to line 2 again. What pair of words forms a similar echo? You won't find anything like this further on, though.

- There are some suggestions of unpleasantness in the lines, too. Potential loss is hinted at – and why is there no hay to be lost?

3 The next sentence runs to the end of line 10 – 'it pummels your house too' – but the balance of emotion has lurched towards fear now.

- How is the idea of desolation – a lack of natural growth – continued in line 5? Think about the poet's choice of words as well as the fact.

- The only idea of comfort here is that the sound of the wind in the trees (which is also the sound of what you fear, though) might distract you from thinking about the attack on your house. Why doesn't it give any comfort? The sound would 'prove company' – so what else haven't 'you' got?

- The strength of the wind is mentioned here for the first time. It's been implied before, though – how? Think about the building of the houses.

- The poet makes the reader think about a sense of fear personally – how?

- Up to line 8, the description is factual, but now imagination starts to work, shown by the speaker starting to use comparisons. What does he compare the sound of the 'gale' to? Why does he choose this comparison, do you think?

- How does the poet emphasise fear in line 9? Think about where the word is placed. Which is the only word to appear twice at the end of a line?

- 'Pummels' is the first word that suggests physical attack by comparing the effect of the storm to being hit. Remember this when you look again at the last six lines.

4 Line 11 is the first sentence to offer no sense of comfort at all. How does the poet emphasise this by the words and ideas in the line? Look carefully at each word, to find as much as you can. It's a very direct statement, too – think about the placement of words on the line, and the punctuation.

5 Look at the next sentence (lines 12–16).

- Lines 12 and 13 contain two ideas which might suggest comfort – what are they? What words suggest that this comfort is false?

- How is it made directly clear at the beginning of line 14 that the comfort is false? Think about the words, where they are placed, and how punctuation emphasises them.

- Pick out the verbs in the sentence, from 'the flung spray' to the end. What do they have in common? Think about what they describe, and how sound links them.

- How does the poet make the attack seem immediate?

- 'Spits like a tame cat / Turned savage'. How does this comparison echo the whole movement of the poem?

6 Now look at the last four lines, which complete the movement of the poem from safety to fear.

- In lines 16–18, pick out the words that compare the storm to a military attack.

- What can 'we' do in the face of this attack? Which word emphasises 'our' helplessness?

- Which two words in these lines prepare for 'nothing' in the last line?

7 What is the 'nothing' that is feared in the last line, do you think? Think about the nature of the force that is attacking, and the island itself, perhaps. How is 'nothing' made fearful by the poet?

8 Look at the first and last words of the last line. How does the poem end, compared with the way it began? How are these words emphasised by placement and punctuation?

Final thoughts

You've done a lot of very detailed work on this poem. Read it through again, trying to pull together everything you've learned. The first eight letters of the poem spell 'Stormont'. Stormont Castle is the main residence of the Secretary of State for Northern Ireland, and has played a key role in Irish politics. You might like to research this, then think why Heaney deliberately chose this opening for a poem about a storm, and how people are affected by it.

Comparisons

You could compare this poem with:

Gillian Clarke
- October
- The Field-Mouse

Pre-1914 Bank
- Patrolling Barnegat
- The Eagle
- Sonnet (Clare)
- Inversnaid

Perch

Read and revise

You should read all the poems you study aloud, to hear how the sounds in the poems work. Often you can do this by 'hearing' the words in your head, and not speaking aloud; but with this poem you'll gain a lot if you say it aloud, or listen to somebody else saying it. Try it, reading slowly so that you can savour each sound. Listen for all the echoes that are created, and how 'everything flows'.

1   As you read the poem, you probably wondered where to breathe, because the poem is one long sentence. Why do you think the poet chose to do this? Think about what he is describing.

2   Sound echoes and connections are made in a number of ways in this poem. Look at the last words of the first two lines of the poem, 'River' and 'waver'. The two words don't form a rhyme, because the vowel sounds are different, but they do echo. Which sound is the same in both words?

3   You can see on the page that the poem is divided into five pairs of lines. Go down looking at each pair of last words, and work out how they echo – you'll quickly see where the same sound is made within each pair.

4   The river is the 'clear Bann'. Where are these two words echoed within the next line? Again, look very carefully at each word to see how the echo is made. Two useful technical terms to use here are alliteration and **assonance**. Alliteration is the repetition of consonant sounds to gain an effect. Assonance is the repetition of vowel sounds to gain an effect. Which terms are used here?

5 Look at line 3. There's an assonance in 'grunts' and 'runty', because the 'u' sound is repeated. The same sound is repeated twice more in the line – find them. Remember not to look just for the same spelling – it's the sound that matters. There are alliterations in the line, too – find them.

6 'I saw and I see' (line 4) is actually the stem of the whole sentence – you could re-order the sentence by putting these words at the beginning. Why do you think the poet chose to put them in the middle? Think about the effect the whole poem is aiming at.

7 'I saw and I see' does more than this, though. What is repeated in the phrase? What rhythm is created? And of course, what word does it make you think of? (Turn it round!)

8 The word 'pass' at the end of line 5 is a repetition of part of a word – find it. The poet is busy playing with the meanings as well as the sounds of words, though. This is the same word, but with different meanings. What does it mean each time?

9 In the same line, 'bluntly' might be a good word to describe the shape and position of the fish as they hold their place in the water, but there's sound going on too. What sound is being echoed here that has already been heard and repeated in the poem?

10 In line 6, how does the poet make you see the position of the perch from their point of view?

11 Pick out the assonances in line 7. Look back to Question 4 to check what you're looking for.

12 'Finland' (line 8) means 'the land of fins', as in fish, here, but there's a play on words too, isn't there? There's a strong echo of the same word in the line, of course. How is this like 'I saw and I see'? Think about rhythm as well as sound.

13 There are repetitions and echoes going on between different parts of the poem, as well as in lines and pairs of lines. Look at line 8 and then back to the first two lines. What echoes and repetitions are there?

14 In this world where everything is mixed up and flows together, even one element of nature can seem like another. Can you find this idea in lines 8 and 9? Where, exactly? How does the poet make the idea stand out by the placement of words, and by verse divisions?

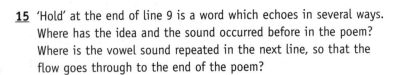

15 'Hold' at the end of line 9 is a word which echoes in several ways. Where has the idea and the sound occurred before in the poem? Where is the vowel sound repeated in the next line, so that the flow goes through to the end of the poem?

16 The 'steady go of the world' (line 10). Whose world?

Final thoughts

The questions you have worked through concentrate mostly on the sounds of the poem, because that is its outstanding feature. Putting the effects together, how has Seamus Heaney created the world of the perch by using these methods?

The poem describes the perch, but from a particular person's point of view – the 'I' of line 4. What do you think is his attitude to the fish? Is it just a neutral description, or does he like them – or what? Find evidence for your response.

Comparisons

You could compare this poem with:

Gillian Clarke
- Cold Knap Lake
- A Difficult Birth . . .

Pre-1914 Bank
- Patrolling Barnegat
- The Eagle
- Sonnet (Clare)
- Inversnaid

Blackberry-Picking

Read and revise

Read the poem right through once, to see where it is going before you start working on it.

1 The poem is about ripe fruit. How does Heaney introduce ripeness in the first two lines? Think about full, round sounds as well as ideas associated with ripeness.

2 What does the phrase 'At first, just one' (line 3) imply about what is to follow?

3 To capture the child's delight in the fruit, the poet uses the senses involved in savouring the fruit. Sight begins in line 3, with 'glossy purple'. Look through lines 3–14, picking out all the references to colour and appearance. Remember that colour might be suggested not just by naming it, but also by using things which have a characteristic colour that we can't help seeing when we picture it. 'Blood' is one example in these lines, but there are more.

4 There's one clear reference in the first six lines to taste. Find it. It's also implied a couple of times. See if you can find these too.

5 Touch is used too. 'Hard as a knot' (line 4) is the first, but there are more in the first 16 lines. Find them.

6 This isn't just a poem describing fruit – it's about how the child felt about picking them, at various stages. 'Lust for / Picking' is a clear example of a feeling about the task. Can you find any words associated with lust? Find another feeling mentioned in the first sixteen lines, and words associated with it.

7 Although there is only one to begin with, a lot of blackberries ripen eventually. The list of containers they use in line 9 implies an abundance. Find more examples of large numbers of berries being implied in lines 10–16.

8 Look at lines 15 and 16. 'Like a plate of eyes' suggests guilt, perhaps, as well as appearance. Can you find any other suggestions of guilt or punishment for crime in these two lines?

9 Now look at the last eight lines. Which word in line 17 suggests a large number?

10 How is the 'fur' made to sound unpleasant in lines 18 and 19? Think about the sound of the words as well as the associations they have.

11 Senses are still used in these lines. Find examples of sight, smell and taste being used. How does Heaney remind you in line 22 that this is a childhood experience being described?

12 Look at the last line. There's a balance in this line, created by the phrasing. Hear how the line sounds, either by saying it in your head or out loud. How is the balance created, exactly?

13 The poem ends on 'not'. They will never keep. To make this idea strong in the reader's mind, the poet has used a number of methods to stress 'not', in addition to making it the last word of the poem. There's a balance in the line – how does 'not' seem to bring the balance down? All of the pairs of lines echo, but only two pairs rhyme fully. Find them. Now think about the effect of 'not' at the end, especially given the earlier full rhyme. Think about repeated sounds, and completion.

Final thoughts

Read the poem through again, noticing all the sense and sounds at work now that you've recognised them. Think about the way the poem shifts from a pleasant experience to a disappointing, even unpleasant one. Where does the change start to happen?

You could compare this poem with:

Comparisons

Gillian Clarke	Pre-1914 Bank
• The Field-Mouse	• Patrolling Barnegat
• A Difficult Birth . . .	• Tichborne's Elegy
• October	• Sonnet (Clare)

Death of a Naturalist

Glossary

flax	a strong-growing plant
flax-dam	a wet area covered with flax
festered	became rotten or decayed
rank	overgrown

Read and revise

The effect of this poem depends quite heavily on the sound of the words that the poet chooses. Read the poem right through at least once, noticing the sound of the words as well as what they mean.

1 The first ten lines of the poem describe the flax-dam. To capture the atmosphere of the place for the reader, the poet refers to four of the senses – sight, sound, touch and smell. Find as many examples of each of these as you can.

2 The picture that the poet paints of the scene in the first ten lines is not a pleasant one. Which word in the first line sets the tone of the place? Can you find any other words in the first ten lines that have a similar meaning?

3 All the elements of the description put together create a very strong atmosphere, and the poet contributes to this by choosing words with similar sounds. There are repetitions of consonant sounds,

called alliteration, and repetitions of vowel sounds, called assonance. 'Heavy headed' in line 2, for instance, has both of these – the 'h' sound is repeated (alliteration), and so is the 'e' sound (assonance). Pick out as many examples of each as you can in the first ten lines.

4 Which vowel sounds seem heavy to you? 'Punishing sun' in line 4 is a start. Which words mean something heavy? 'Weighted down' in line 3 is a start.

5 Now look for words that suggest heat, and words that suggest thickness.

6 Looking at everything you have found so far, what can you say about the atmosphere that the poet has created?

7 Eventually the speaker comes to dislike this place, but before the event described at the end of the poem he seems to like it. Which phrase suggests that he likes it? Notice that this is the first time that it is clear that this is a personal poem.

8 Look at the sentence that runs from line 10 to line 15, from 'Here, every spring' to 'Swimming tadpoles'.

- What is the poet describing here?

- The tone of the poem has changed. Look at 'nimble- / Swimming' (lines 14–15). Which vowel sound is repeated here? Can you find more uses of the same sound in these five lines? How is this sound different from the sounds used in the first ten lines of the poem?

9 Now look at the rest of the first section, from 'Miss Walls' (line 15) to 'In rain' (line 21). Think about how the poet conveys the way Miss Walls talked to the children.

- Which describing words reflect the words she would have used?

- How does the form of the sentence reflect the form she would she have used? (Think about the way 'and' is used, for instance).

- What is there in the last sentence of the section that reflects the way the infant teacher would speak?

10 The poem is about a change of attitude. The change in the poem is emphasised by the break in the poem after line 21. How does the poet underline this break? Think about:

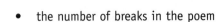

- the number of breaks in the poem
- the length of line 21
- the beginning of line 22.

11 The change is also marked by a return to the language of an adult looking back on the childhood experience, rather than the language of the child and the teacher. How have the words and the sentences changed?

12 The sounds of the words have returned to the sounds that dominated the first ten lines, too. 'Coarse croaking' repeats a 'c' sound, for instance. Look through the lines after the break to the end of the poem for alliteration and assonance, noticing what sort of sounds occur most often.

13 The sense of sound, smell, sight and touch are used again, too. Look through the same lines, picking out as many examples of each as you can.

14 The day of the event is 'hot'. How does this add to the unpleasantness of the atmosphere and the event?

15 'Rank' means overgrown, but also rotting and foul.
- Which other words in these lines suggest either of these ideas, of things being either too big, or horrible, or both?
- Look for words that suggest weight again.

16 The frogs are described as 'angry' (line 23). Which other words in these lines suggest an aggressive attitude?

17 'Invaded' (line 24) is a military word. Can you find any other words that belong to war?

18 The frogs are described as 'The great slime kings' (line 31). How else is sliminess suggested in these lines? Look for words that suggest sliminess, and for sounds too (line 29, for instance).

19 How does the poet convey the strength of the speaker's fear and revulsion? Look at line 31.

20 The last line shows how much the speaker's attitude has changed from the feeling in the first ten lines. What was 'best of all' (line 8)? How have things changed completely?

Final thoughts

How has the poet prepared the reader for the feeling of revulsion that overcomes the speaker at the end of the poem? Think about all the things you found in the last section.

The poem is called 'Death of a Naturalist'. Why?

Comparisons

You could compare this poem with:

Gillian Clarke
- The Field-Mouse
- A Difficult Birth . . .
- Cold Knap Lake

Pre-1914 Bank
- Patrolling Barnegat
- Sonnet (Clare)

Digging

Read and revise

Read the poem right through once. The last line, 'I'll dig with it', makes you think about the whole poem again. Read it through again, thinking about what the last line means – there may be more than one thing. If you're writing notes, don't write anything down about this yet – wait till you've worked through the questions below.

1 Look at the first two lines.

- The opening picture of the poet's pen compares it to 'a gun'. What does this suggest about how the poet thinks he might write?

- The word 'snug' suggests something that fits comfortably in the hand. How does this fit the nature of the writer? The poet uses sounds to add to this idea of 'fitting together'. What sound is repeated twice in these lines – and placed where you'll hear it clearly? Repetition of vowel sounds to gain an effect is called assonance.

2 The poem suggests that the father and grandfather are in harmony with their work, that their actions fit the purpose of digging. Look at the next three lines (lines 3–5). In the first two lines it was the repetition of vowel sounds that joined things together. Look at these three lines for repetition of consonant sounds. This is called alliteration. How many can you find? (You should find two.)

3 What is the speaker doing at the beginning of the poem, do you think? Where **exactly** does he start thinking about the past rather than listening to what he can hear in the present?

4 In the next five lines (10–14) the verbs the poet uses are significant. Find all the verbs in the lines (notice how many are used here). Think now about the action of digging, which needs to be clean and sharp. How do the verbs and their sounds help create this idea?

5 How does the poet make lines 15 and 16 stand out? (Look at the page.) What the speaker says here is very simple. How does the poet use form (think about what you've just done) and language to emphasise its simplicity?

6 Lines 15 and 16 show how the speaker admires his father and grandfather.

- Look right through the poem, finding more evidence of his admiration for these men.

- Some of the admiration is implied rather than stated directly – for instance, in lines 17–21 the first line is obviously admiration – but what can you find in lines 20 and 21?

7 Look at lines 22–24. The poem begins to draw together in these lines.

- Look at the verbs in line 22, and consider what you found in the answer to Question 4. How else is 'clean and sharp' conveyed in this line?

- Is any admiration conveyed in these lines? How?

- Everything from line 5 to line 24 is described in one word here. What is it? How does the poet emphasise the word by punctuation and placement in the line? How does the break between stanzas help?

- The poem seems to come to a stop at the end of line 24. What has been completed? Look at the next four lines, and think about time and what is happening now.

8 The next four lines, 25–28, sum up what the speaker has remembered, and prepare for the final thought.

- How do lines 25 and 26 include both his father and grandfather?

- These two lines contain alliteration, like lines 3 and 4. Find the repeated consonants.

- 'Through living roots awaken in my head' (line 27). What are the 'living roots', do you think? Don't be satisfied with one meaning!

- How do the roots 'awaken in my head'? Remember there is more than one meaning to 'roots', so there may be more than one meaning to this.

- What is the poet saying about himself in line 28? What is his attitude to the 'men', and how is it conveyed?

9 'I'll dig with it.'

- This has two meanings. In one sense, the poet has been 'digging' within himself throughout the poem. What does this mean? Think about who he describes, and 'going down and down / For the good turf', and 'living roots'.

- The poet's work is to 'dig' with a pen – it is the tool to use in his job. In this sense, the poem is a result of an act of 'digging', isn't it? For example, 'nicking and slicing neatly' with a spade might be like carefully deciding on line and verse breaks in a poem like this. What other comparisons can you find? Think about all the methods the poet uses here, which are the way he 'digs'.

10 The last three lines bring the poem full circle by repeating the opening phrase – but this also highlights the change, from 'gun' to 'spade'. How does this indicate how the poet sees himself, and the writing of poetry, do you think?

Final thoughts

Read through the poem one last time, thinking about more ways in which Seamus Heaney has 'dug' the poem. What might 'the good turf' be, apart from turf itself?

Comparisons	You could compare this poem with:	
	Gillian Clarke	**Pre-1914 Bank**
	• Catrin	• Sonnet 130
	• Mali	• The Affliction of Margaret
	• October	• Song of the Old Mother
		• Sonnet (Clare)

Mid-Term Break

g

> **Glossary**
>
> **knelling**   the sound of a bell ringing, especially to signal death or a funeral
>
> **starched**   made to stop bleeding

Read and revise

Read the poem through once. It's apparently a very simple poem – notice how simple the sentences and statements are as you read.

1 Why does the poet choose to use the word 'knelling' instead of 'ringing' in line 2? Think of the tone that the word starts to create in the reader's mind, not just the meaning.

2 Apart from the word 'knelling', the first three lines are very simple and factual – just statements of what happened. How are they made to seem so simple? Think about the shape of the sentences, and the number of sentences in three lines. Think too about the effect of the end-stopped lines – these are lines of verse with a full stop at the end.

3 In lines 4–6, find two examples of things being unusually sad and affecting – one stated, one implied.

4 In such a simple account, details are obviously very carefully chosen. The one detail that seems to have nothing to do with the sad events is 'The baby cooed and laughed and rocked the pram' (line 7). Why do you think the poet chooses this detail? Think about the contrast between this and the child described in the last five lines. Think about the effect of the cluster of verbs in the line.

5 Look at lines 8–13, from 'I was embarrassed' to 'angry tearless sighs'.

- What do you learn about the family here?

- How is grief stated or implied here?

- The speaker is the centre of attention here. How does he feel about this? How do you know?

6 Look at lines 14 and 15.

- Again, this is a simple statement of the event. How is it made to seem so? Look at Question 2 again.

- The time is mentioned here, for the second time in the poem. Find the first (and notice where it is in the sentence, if you haven't before, which makes this seem like a repetition). Now glance through the rest of the poem to find the other mentions of the time, or time having passed. Why do you think the poet mentions time so much at the end? Think about time stopping, as well as time passing.

7 The words and sentences become a little less simple now.

- How is the form of the sentence that runs from line 16 to line 18 slightly more complex than what has gone before?

- 'Snowdrops / And candles soothed the bedside'. Why do you think the poet chooses to mention this detail? What are the associations that these things have? The word 'soothed' is not factual. Why do you think the poet chooses this word?

8 The sentence that runs from 'Paler now' (line 18) to 'as in his cot' (line 20) is still less simple.

- How is the form of the sentence less simple than what has gone before? Look at the beginning of the sentence, and where the main verb comes, compared to the other sentences. How is the different beginning emphasised as you say it by the break between one stanza and the next?

- Time is important in the poem. The word 'now' is emphasised by being placed at the end of a line, just before the stanza break. Why, do you think? Think about what is happening in the speaker's account of events, and the time that has passed, and what has happened.

- 'Wearing a poppy bruise' (line 19). Such a strong comparison stands out in a poem where nearly all the statements are factual. Why does the poet choose this comparison? Think about the colour. Think also about when a poppy is worn – and the poet clearly intends you to think of this because of the choice of the word 'wearing'.

9 He lay 'as in his cot' (line 20). Why does the poet use this detail? Think of the difference between his cot and this box, which the similarity brings out. Think about the baby in line 7, too.

10 Now look at the last two lines, which complete the poem's effect.

- The child's age is withheld until the last word of the poem. Why, do you think?

- There is a return to simple statements here. Notice the end-stopped lines again – two on the run for the first time. Look for the verbs in the lines, to see how a final simplicity is emphasised.

- Why is the last line separate, do you think? Notice it is the only line like this in the poem, which increases the effect.

- The final word, 'year', which is so important to the overall effect on the reader, is emphasised further by the repeated 'ear' sound, created by the full rhyme with 'clear'. This is particularly strong because it's the first rhyme of any sort in the poem. Why has the poet chosen not to use rhyme, do you think? The effect at the end might be one reason, and it adds to the sense of simplicity – but can you think of any other reason? Think about the nature of what is being described.

Final thoughts

The questions have encouraged you to see how the poet creates simplicity in the poem, and where he moves away from it. Read the poem again. Why do you think the poet has chosen this simple style for this subject?

Think about the title. Why do you think the poet chose this title? Think of as many reasons as you can, not just a simple one!

Comparisons

You could compare this poem with:

Gillian Clarke	**Pre-1914 Bank**
• Cold Knap Lake	• On my first Sonne
• On the Train	• The Little Boy Lost / The Little Boy Found
• Mali	• Tichborne's Elegy

Follower

Read and revise

Read the poem through once, focusing on the speaker's attitude to his father.

1 Look at the first verse (lines 1–4). This appears to be a simple description, but it's not as simple as it looks.

- The first line is simple – what makes it so? Think about the shape of the sentence.

- A clear picture is painted by the poet's words in lines 2 and 3 – try to see in your mind the exact picture. What does 'globed' tell you about the father's shoulders? 'Like a full sail' might conjure up the same sort of shape – but it's 'strung / Between the shafts and the furrow'. Think about the shape he forms with the plough and the land. If you don't know what the horse-plough looks like, you need to find a picture of a man working one, to see what the poet is describing.

- How is the father's control of the horses emphasised in line 4? Which word says the most about his control?

2   Look at lines 5–7.

- 'An expert' is a simple summary of what the father is in his job. How does the poet make this stand out, so that the reader feels it as a summation of what he is? Think about the number of words used, and where they appear in the line and in the verse – and what they come after.

- Look at the verbs in lines 5 and 6. How do they show expertise?

- How is expertise shown in line 7?

3   Look at the sentence beginning 'At the headrig' (line 8), and ending 'back into the land' (line 10).

- How is the father's control over the team conveyed? Think about the contrast between the man and the animals.

- The 'single pluck' is one sharp movement. How does the poet make the reader feel this? Think about the sound of the word, combined with where it is on the line, and where the verse division comes.

4   In the rest of this verse, 'His eye' (line 10) to 'the furrow exactly' (line 12), how is the father's precision emphasised? Look at the verbs as well as the obvious word.

5   Look at the next verse (lines 13–16).

- How is the boy, following behind, different to the father? Pick out the two words that make the difference clear.

- The boy follows 'in his . . . wake' (line 13). What is the father in front being compared to? What does this remind you of in the poem? Look back to the first verse.

- The rhythm of the lines in the poem isn't always regular, but line 16 is. Why has the poet made it so regular and steady?

<u>**6**</u>   Look at lines 17–20, which give the boy's attitude to his father.

- How are you reminded in this verse that the speaker is remembering himself as a child?

- The boy wanted to copy his father, so he must have admired him. Find all the words in the poem that suggest that the boy admired the father in his work.

- How is it suggested in this verse that the boy never did become a farmer, even though he wanted to 'follow' him?

<u>**7**</u>   Now look at the last verse, where the poem both ends and changes.

- The whole poem to this point has been about the past that the adult remembers. Where exactly does the change to the present come, and how is it marked?

- The last two lines suggest that the situations of child and father have been reversed. What do you think the poet means by saying that the father is 'stumbling / Behind' him and 'will not go away'? There could be several meanings. For one meaning, it might help to read Heaney's poem **Digging**. What is the grown-up child's work, and what does he keep thinking about?

Final thoughts

Now read the poem again, thinking about the title. There are two 'followers' in this poem. In what senses are they 'followers'? There may be more than one for each, of course.

You could compare this poem with:

Gillian Clarke	Pre-1914 Bank
• Catrin	• On my first Sonne
• Mali	• The Affliction of Margaret
• Baby-sitting	• The Song of the Old Mother
	• The Little Boy Lost / The Little Boy Found

Comparisons

At a Potato Digging

g

> **Glossary**
>
> | | |
> |---|---|
> | **wicker creels** | baskets made from woven sticks |
> | **homage** | honour or worship |
> | **grafted** | joined on to an established growing plant |
> | **libation** | the act of pouring a liquid as a sacrifice to a god |

Read and revise

Before you read this poem, it's useful to know that in 1845 Ireland was hit by the Great Potato Famine, in which millions of people died from hunger as a result of the outbreak of potato blight.

Now read the poem through once, registering where the poem changes from past to present, then back again.

1 The first section is clearly set in the present. How do you know this from the first line? There are two pieces of evidence.

2 Look at the first verse.

- In the poem the present scene contains reminders of the past. Which words in the first verse suggest death or destruction, even though that's not what they're describing in the present?

- The drill 'Spins up a dark shower of roots and mould' (line 2). The words you have just found help to set up the tone of the poem. This line helps to set the idea of the poem, and its structure. What 'dark shower of roots' appears in the poem from the potato drill? Think about the time change later.

3 Look at the next six lines, from 'Like crows' (line 5) to 'the crumbled surf' (line 10), which describe the labourers.

- This is a description of labourers working together in the present, but the words used to describe them contain echoes and suggestions of the victims of the famine described in section III. For instance, 'Like crows' (line 5) compares the labourers to birds. Where do you find a similar comparison in section III? Find as many examples as you can, working backwards and forwards between the descriptions. This will take some time to do, but it's evidence of one of the points of the poem – how the present contains reminders of the past.

- The labourers work together. The poet uses repetition of sounds to echo this 'joined together' feeling. For instance, look at the number of words that begin with 'h' in line 6 (repetition of consonant sounds is called alliteration). Find as any repetitions of sounds, either consonants or vowels (assonance) in these lines as you can.

- The labourers stand for 'a moment' (line 9). How does the break between the second and third verse create the moment? Say it aloud.

4 Now look at the end of the first section, from 'Heads bow' (line 11) to 'altar of the sod' (line 16). There is an important idea introduced in these lines.

- Find all the references you can to religion in these lines. Think about words, and physical positions and attitudes.

- What is the god at the heart of this religious idea? Look at line 16, and at the first word of line 12. What is the 'Mother'? Maybe the capital letter isn't just because it's the first word of the line – that merely helps to identify what it is. If the labourers are imagined as being like people praying, what are they praying for, and what do they fear?

5 The second section describes the potatoes themselves.

- In lines 17–23, how does the poet make these potatoes seem healthy? Think about colour, and what they are compared to. Think too about how they are made to seem harmonious – look for the repetitions of sound, as you did when working on Question 3.

- How are the potatoes made to seem healthy and good in lines 24–29? Think about touch, taste, smell and anything else you can find.

- 'Live skulls, blind-eyed' (line 29) describes the appearance of the potatoes by comparing them to skulls. What physical features are conjured up for the reader? However, the comparison does more than this. The phrase links the present and the past, because it's repeated straight away, at the beginning of the third section. When the phrase is repeated, though, its nature has changed. The first time it's a comparison. What does it describe the second time it is used?

6 The first verse of the third section is a statement of what happened in 1845, and sets the agenda for the section.

- The idea of the starving people's heads as 'live skulls' isn't quite literal – but what does it say about their appearance, and what does it suggest about them?

- How do the verbs 'scoured' and 'wolfed' connect with the skulls?

- The poem is full of echoes between the past and the present. Which word in line 31 connects with the second verse of the first section?

7 There are more echoes in the next two verses. How does the description of the potato in line 34 connect with the first two lines of the second section? How does the comparison in lines 38–41 connect with the second verse of the first section?

8 Look at the comparisons with a bird, in lines 39–41. Why are the faces of the starving likened to 'a plucked bird'? The 'beaks' (line 41) are different – they don't belong to people. What are they the beaks of, and how do they 'snip at guts'?

9 In lines 42–45, the people are compared to plants. How are the people like plants, in lines 42–44? Just as in lines 38–41, the comparison shifts. What is compared to a plant in line 45? How do you think it 'rotted'?

10 Look at lines 46–49, which end the third section.

- How does the poet stress the nastiness of the potato rot in lines 46 and 47?

- What does the poet use to bring the poem back to the present at the end of the section? How do the verbs mark the time shift?

11 If you look back at the first section, which describes the present, you'll see that the first and third lines of each verse rhyme, and the second and fourth. They're mostly full rhymes, too. In the third section, though, which describes 1845, the rhymes are on different lines. Find where. Are they full rhymes, mostly, or half rhymes and echoes? Why do you think the poet chose to use a different scheme for the two sections? Why these choices?

12 Look at lines 50–53.

- How does the content and sound of line 50 mark an immediate change in the mood of the poem?

- What is there in the rest of these four lines that suggests a great difference between the past and present? Think about things, word associations, colours and plenty.

- There are some reminders of the past too, though. Which words are reminders of the grim past?

13 Look at the last verse (lines 54–57).

- As in the last question, what is there in the rest of these four lines that suggests a great difference between the past and present? Think about things, word associations, and plenty.

- Why do you think their fasts are described as 'timeless'? There are several meanings, especially when you think about the past events on this ground.

- Which words in these lines remind you of the end of section 1? Look back to Question 4.

- Why do you think the ground is described as 'faithless'? Think about the rewards the labourers of 1845 received. How were they 'stretched on the . . . ground'?

14 The time line of the poem has come full circle. Think about the title now. How does it establish the setting and time in which the action takes place?

Final thoughts

This is the longest and most complex of the poems in the Seamus Heaney selection. Read it through again carefully, noting the links the poet makes between past and present. You may well find some new ones.

Comparisons

You could compare this poem with:

Gillian Clarke
- A Difficult Birth . . .
- The Field-Mouse

Pre-1914 Bank
- Inversnaid
- Patrolling Barnegat

Gillian Clarke

a Gillian Clarke was born and brought up in Cardiff, and is one of the best-known Welsh poets writing today. Much of her poetry reflects her strong sense of cultural identity. She now lives in a remote cottage in West Wales, where she works as a freelance writer and teacher.

Catrin

Read and revise

1 The first line establishes a number of important things about the poem.

- There are two people involved in the poem. Which personal pronouns are used to identify them here?

- Which word in the line establishes the relationship between the two?

2 Look at lines 6–9.

- Find the line that repeats almost exactly the first line. In this line, 'I' and 'you' are almost like opposites. Which word gives the reader the first idea that the two are joined together in some way?

- Find other words in these lines which suggest togetherness, and words which suggest conflict – and the one word which says how they feel about each other.

- These words suggest two people who are joined closely together, but still fight. What physical thing are they joined by?

3 Find the three descriptions of the place where the action is set.

- 'White', 'blank', 'glass tank'. What is this room, do you think, and how do the descriptions show what the speaker thinks about it?

- Look at line 10. There are two other words here which make the room seem impersonal. What are they?

- Look at lines 11–14. How does the speaker 'colour' the walls? Look carefully at what she 'writes' and colours with.

4 Look at lines 14–17.

- Which words are about, or imply, conflict?

- Which words or phrases suggest being apart?

- What does 'ourselves' imply? How does the poet set out the poem to draw your attention to this word?

5 Lines 18–20 mark a change in the poem.

- Line 18 is still in the past tense – but how do we know that the poet is looking back on the events described in the first section?

- How does Clarke show that the events described between the end of line 20 and the end of the poem have moved forward in time? Which word tells you this?

- Which word in the line tells you that nothing has changed?

6 There's still conflict between the two. Find the words in lines 20–29 that suggest conflict.

7 Look at the description of the daughter in lines 22–24.

- What does the mother admire about her daughter?

- Look at the words she chooses – and listen to them. Which sounds are repeated? What effect does the repetition have?

8 When the mother looks at the daughter, and listens to her request, 'that old rope' is brought up from 'the heart's pool'.

- What is the rope? It's not physical rope here.

- It's an 'old' rope now. Dating back to when?

- The rope is first described as a 'tight' rope, and here it is 'Tightening about my life'. Why is it 'tight', do you think? Will it ever let go?

9 The feeling is brought on by the look on the girl's face, but also by her simple request. Why should this bring out 'love and conflict'?

10 'May you skate / In the dark, for one more hour' (line 29). What else do you think the poet might mean by this, apart from the simple request? Think about the young child as well as the older one.

Final thoughts

Read the poem through again, taking in all the ideas about love and conflict. You might like to think about one more detail – the first thing Gillian Clarke describes. She watches 'people and cars taking / Turn at the traffic lights'.

Why did she choose to include this detail in this short poem about mother and daughter, do you think? The 'rope' is red, too – maybe for more than just one reason. Think about what this might link up with.

Comparisons

You could compare this poem with:

Seamus Heaney
- Follower
- Digging

Pre-1914 Bank
- The Affliction of Margaret
- On my first Sonne
- The Song of the Old Mother

Baby-sitting

Read and revise

Read the poem through once, noticing how simple and straightforward most of the statements are.

<u>1</u> Look at the shape of the statements in the first stanza (there are three statements in the sentence beginning 'She is sleeping'). What makes them seem simple? What sort of tone is created by these sentence shapes? Think about the sort of sentences that might have been used if a mother's love was being expressed.

<u>2</u> What isn't right in the first sentence?

<u>3</u> The second sentence, 'I don't love / This baby', is a simple statement of the problem here. What effect does the little pause created by the line break have? Which baby might she love?

<u>4</u> The next sentence, beginning 'She is sleeping', lists the reasons why the baby might be loved. How does 'a perfectly acceptable child' suggest that it isn't loved by the babysitter?

<u>5</u> Look at the rest of the first stanza, from 'I am afraid' to 'fail to enchant me' (line 10).

- Find all the words in these lines that state or imply the babysitter's feelings, and the baby's feelings. How are these feelings different from those that might be expected between a mother and child?

- What is the babysitter's attitude to the baby? Find evidence for your answer.

6 'To her I will represent absolute / Abandonment' (lines 11–12). Why will the baby think it has been abandoned? How does the poet emphasise the word 'abandonment'? Think about where the word is on the line, punctuation, and the effect of the line break.

7 Look at the next sentence, from 'For her' (line 12) to 'the terminal ward' (line 16). In this sentence the poet emphasises the baby's sense of abandonment by comparing it to other instances of people feeling abandoned.

- What is similar about the situations of the three people referred to as feeling abandoned? Think about where they each are.

- Much of the first stanza is unemotional. How are these two situations emotional, and what words does the poet use to make them seem emotional?

8 What 'monstrous land' (line 17) do you think the baby is rising from? What 'milk-familiar comforting' (line 18) will she be stretching for?

9 Look at the last two lines.

- How does the poet emphasise that the babysitter feels that there is something missing, which 'will not come'?

- What 'will not come', do you think? Think about what the baby requires physically and emotionally, and what the babysitter would like to feel too.

Final thoughts

Read the poem again, taking in how the whole poem works up to the last line.

Comparisons	You could compare this poem with:	
	Seamus Heaney	**Pre-1914 Bank**
	• Follower	• The Affliction of Margaret
	• Digging	• On my first Sonne
	• Mid-Term Break	• The Song of the Old Mother

Mali

> **Glossary**
> **Mali** is a Welsh girl's name

Read and revise

Mali is taken from a series of poems with the title 'Blood'. This might help you to unpick some of the ideas in the poem. It is apparently a simple poem, but there are some really interesting ideas built into it. Read the poem through once, sorting out the times when the events described in the poem take place.

1 Look at the first sentence, from the beginning to 'I'd thought was over' (line 3).

- The two times described in the poem are set here – now (at the time of writing) and when?

- When does 'that unmistakable . . . tug of the tide' happen – now or in the past? If it's difficult to decide, perhaps that's deliberate.

- 'The tide' is a key idea in the poem. Just notice it here – later in the poem you'll need to think what it might mean. It doesn't just mean a sea tide here, though, does it?

2 Look at the next sentence, from 'I drove (line 3) to 'so slowly home' (line 7).

- Which time period does the journey described here belong to? The tense of the verb in line 3 should help you.

- The poem is full of ideas about time – tides, seasons, too soon / too late. Here time seems to pass slowly. Which words in these lines suggest or state that things are happening slowly? Think about the sound of words as well as their meaning.

- The daughter, however, wants to move quickly. Why? What is going to happen?

3 Look at the next five lines, from 'Something in the event' (line 8) to 'our fingers purple' (line 12).

- These lines are packed with references to seasons and ripeness. Find as many as you can, thinking about each word.

- Colours are also stated or implied here several times. Again, find all the references.

- Now think about what you've just found. How are these ideas of colour and ripeness associated with what is happening to the daughter and the mother? Remember the title of the series of poems.

4   Now look at the next four lines, which complete the sentence, from 'then the child' (line 13) to 'a harvest moon' (line 16).

- These lines are packed with references to time. Find all the references you can.

- How has the child come 'too soon' and 'in the wrong place'?

- After the stanza break at the end of line 14, the next two lines reflect on the birth, at the end of the day, perhaps. What in the day has been 'seasonal' and what 'out of season'?

- In line 16, what suggests that this is the end of the day? Which word connects with the 'tide' of the opening sentence, and the 'beach' of the next sentence? This will tell you why the poet chose to use this exact word.

5   Look at the rest of the third stanza, from 'My daughter's' (line 17) to 'draw me from her' (line 21).

- The baby comes 'too soon' (line 14) but is also a 'late-comer' (line 19). How is she a 'late-comer'? The poet has deliberately chosen to play with the idea of something being out of its 'seasonal' time, in the confusion of 'soon' and 'late'.

- As the grandmother looks at the child on the beach, how is she 'hooked' again, do you think? Why has the poet chosen this word? Think about the tide again, and where this takes place.

- She is 'life-sentenced'. What do you think this means? Think about how the grandmother feels about the child, her 'daughter's daughter', and think about the word 'life', too.

- 'Even the sea could not draw me from her' simply describes the pull of the child – it's all she could look at. But the words the poet chooses make the reader think of other things, too. How else does the sea 'draw' things? Look at the first sentence again.

6   Look at the next sentence, from 'This year' (line 22) to 'streamers' (line 24).

- What sort of activity is baking a cake? Try to relate it to the rest of the poem. The cake is like 'our house'. What has this to do with the relationships described in the poem, and the threesome in both time periods?

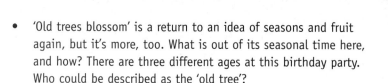

- 'Old trees blossom' is a return to an idea of seasons and fruit again, but it's more, too. What is out of its seasonal time here, and how? There are three different ages at this birthday party. Who could be described as the 'old tree'?

7 Now look at the last sentence, from 'we celebrate' to the end.

- Why do you think the poet compares what they drink to 'the cold blue ocean'? What idea, which is present throughout the poem, appears again?

- There is a sense in the last two lines of things drawing to a close. How does the poet achieve this? Look at the words and think about their associations.

- There are three drops of blood. Why three? What unites the people at the celebration?

- What do you think the 'last blood' in the last line means? There are various possibilities – think of as many as you can. It may help to think about the ideas of tides and seasons which have run throughout the poem, and so might prepare you for the ending. Now is the time to look back and think about the first sentence again. What did the grandmother think 'was over'?

Final thoughts

You can probably see now that this a much more rich and complex poem than it appears to be at first. Read it through again, noticing how the poet manages to make simple things contain more complex ideas, and how complexity is made simple.

Comparisons	You could compare this poem with:	
	Seamus Heaney	**Pre-1914 Bank**
	• Follower	• The Affliction of Margaret
	• Digging	• On my first Sonne
	• Blackberry-Picking	• The Song of the Old Mother
		• Sonnet (Clare)

A Difficult Birth, Easter 1998

g | **Glossary**
Good Friday	Christ was crucified on Good Friday
The Good Friday Agreement	an agreement reached at Easter 1998, setting up a framework for peace in Northern Ireland
Easter 1916	the date of the Easter Rising, in Dublin. Its aim was to destroy British rule and establish an independent Irish republic.

Read and revise

In the Christian religion, Christ is often referred to as 'a Lamb'. Christ was crucified on Good Friday. On Easter Sunday the rock covering the mouth of his tomb was found rolled away. Christ had risen from the dead. The poem likens the lamb's birth to the hope for the future promised by the Good Friday Agreement. Read the poem, looking for the parallels which the poet finds between the two events.

1   Look at the first verse, which sets up the situation for the reader.

- The Irish problem had seemed hopeless for many years. How is the old ewe's situation made to seem similar? What has seemed impossible?

- In lines 3 and 4, how has the poet linked the two events? What two things are 'close'? Think about the shape of the sentence, too – what is the effect of 'and'? How might the attitudes of the ewe also apply to the participants in the peace talks?

- The 'quiet supper and bottle of wine' in line 5 seem to be just a casual detail. How might they connect with the last days and death of Christ? You might have to do some research.

2   Now look at the second verse.

- Each verse moves the time on a little. How has it moved on here?

- Look carefully at the words 'exhausted, tamed by pain' in line 10. How does the poet make these words apply to both situations? Look where they are in the sentence, and think how you can read them two ways.

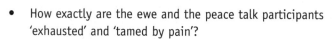

- How exactly are the ewe and the peace talk participants 'exhausted' and 'tamed by pain'?

- 'Two hooves and a muzzle' means that the lamb is partly born, but stuck. How might this describe the progress of the talks at that moment, do you think?

3 In the third verse (lines 13–18), how has the situation got worse, or at least no better? What might be the equivalent in the talks?

4 In the first sentence of the last verse, which words emphasise the difficulty of the process? How might this describe the progress of the talks at that moment, do you think? Which repeated word suggests hope, though? How?

5 Now look at the last sentence, from 'She drinks him' (line 21) to the end, which brings the poem to a miraculous conclusion.

- 'Peaceful' clearly signals the parallel between the outcomes of the two situations. How does the poet emphasise the word by punctuation and placement on the line?

- 'At a cradling that might have been a death.' How do the two possible outcomes stated here apply to both situations?

- The word 'cradling', though, suggests the reader might think about the story of Christ again. How? How does the whole phrase also apply to the story of Easter?

- The word 'lamb' is used in line 23 for only the second time in the poem – surprisingly, as the whole poem is about a lambing. Why does the poet use it here? What does she want the reader to associate the lamb with?

- What is the ewe's 'opened door'? How might the phrase also apply to the story of the resurrection, and to the peace agreement?

- 'The stone rolled away,' the final phrase of the poem, is the moment of miracle. How does the poet lift the whole phrase out of the poem, so that the reader is left with a surprise, almost? Look at the shape of the poem on the page.

- How does 'the stone rolled away' apply to each of the three situations? The 'stone' is literal in the story of Christ – what is it in the other two situations.

Final thoughts

Read the poem again. There are three situations in the poet's and the reader's mind by the end of the poem. Which situation is most in your mind at the end of the poem? Why?

Comparisons

You could compare this poem with:

Seamus Heaney

- At a Potato Digging
- Mid-Term Break

Pre-1914 Bank

- Sonnet (Clare)
- On my first Sonne
- Inversnaid
- Tichborne's Elegy

The Field-Mouse

g

Glossary

snare drum	a small side drum, usually for military use
the radio's terrible news	refers to the 'ethnic cleansing' in Bosnia that happened during the civil war, when neighbours fought neighbours
lime	a white chemical spread on land to increase fertility

Read and revise

This poem was written at the time of the Bosnia-Herzogovina conflict in Europe. It is set at harvest time on a farm, but is about the war in Europe. Read the poem through once, noticing how the words keep referring to the war, sometimes directly and sometimes indirectly.

1 Read the first verse again. It sets the scene for the poem.

- There are two direct references to the war in this verse. Find them.

- What is mentioned in line 1 which you might associate with war?

- How do the people working in the meadow try to escape from thoughts of war?

- What are they doing which might still remind them of war? How does the poet make the action seem war-like?

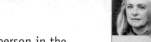

- The word 'neighbour' (line 7) implies that the person in the adjoining territory is friendly – very unlike a field of war. How do the neighbour's actions reinforce this impression? Which particular words suggest that the neighbour's actions are not harmful?

2   Look again at the second verse, which contains the action in the poem.

- Which word in line 10 is a reminder of destruction?

- There are two lines about the mouse's eyes. What are the eyes compared to? Think about the colour of the eyes before and after death. What is the effect of the light going out, therefore? What's left? Why this colour?

- 'It curls in agony as big as itself' (line 14). What does 'big as itself' imply about the mouse's pain?

3   The last three lines of the verse, from 'Summer in Europe' to 'what we have crushed' (line 18), extend the scope of the poem.

- 'In Europe', although it applies to the field they're in, makes the reader think of the 'terrible news' (line 4) from elsewhere. What sort of 'field' might be 'hurt' elsewhere?

- How is it clear in line 17 that the speaker is thinking about more than just her child with the dead mouse?

- 'We' in line 13 clearly refers to the people cutting hay – but if these three lines are about the wider conflict, who are the 'we' in line 18, do you think? Think about the contrast with the 'children' in line 17, and perhaps the reader too – you. What is being said about responsibility here?

4   Look again at the next six lines, from 'Before day's done' (line 19) to 'we can't face the newspapers' (line 23).

- The field was 'hurt' (line 16), and now it's 'bleeding'. What is the field being compared to? How does it increase the sense of hurt and damage? How might this also make you think of the field in Europe?

- The 'wrong' (line 21) is clearly tied to the war in Europe, not the hay field. How do you know this?

- The idea of injury – 'hurt' and 'bleeding' – is continued here. Where, exactly? How is the sense of injury made to appear even worse than before?

<u>5</u> Now read the last four lines, from 'All night I dream'
(line 24) to the end. The first verse, despite its warning notes, is
a peaceful scene set on the speaker's farm. In the dream, all this
is changed.

- Dreams – or nightmares, rather – transform what happens in
  our ordinary lives. Where, in what has actually happened, might
  the sight of children dancing have come from?

- In this nightmare, what do the children seem like? How are
  they made to seem vulnerable?

- How do these two details – the dancing and the description of
  bones – add to the sense of the damage inflicted by war?

- What does the word 'stammering' (line 26) sound like? (When a
  word is used which has the same sound as the thing it is
  describing, this is called onomatopoeia.) How is the word
  emphasised by its position in the line?

- The 'neighbour' in the first verse is clearly kind. How has he
  changed in the dream? Which word tells you? Notice the
  position of the word in the line, too.

- In the place where they live, the neighbour gives them
  'sweetness'. In the dream, which word describes the nature of
  his actions? How does this connect with the idea that runs
  through the poem from line 16 to the end?

Final thoughts

What have the field, and the mouse, and the child come to
represent in the poem? Read it through again.

The poet has chosen to structure this poem in three verses, each
one developing the meaning of the poem. The first verse sets the
scene, and in the second the action – the child bringing the
dying mouse – takes place. What is the third verse about?
What does it do?

Comparisons

You could compare this poem with:

Seamus Heaney
- Blackberry-Picking
- Death of a Naturalist
- At a Potato Digging

Pre-1914 Bank
- The Man He Killed
- Sonnet (Clare)
- Patrolling Barnegat

October

> **Glossary**
>
> **poplars**   trees with bright green leaves that turn brown in autumn
>
> **lobelia**   a trailing plant, whose flowers are often blue
>
> **orcop**   a small village in Hertfordshire
>
> **laurels and** shrubs
> **hydrangeas**

Read and revise

Read the poem through once, then think about the shape
of the whole poem before you go on to the questions below.
The poem is divided into three verses. What is the first verse
about? The second? The third?

1   The poem is partly about the movement of time, and death.
How are these things suggested in the first sentence, even though
the sentence describes wind and trees?

2   'Five poplars / tremble gradually to gold' (lines 2–3). What does
the change in colour indicate? Think about what the poem
is about.

3   How is the rain made to seem sudden in line 4? Think about the
sound of the words as well as what they mean. Repetition of
consonant sounds for effect is called alliteration.

4   Like the description of the trees in lines 1–3, the picture of
the lobelias growing over the head of the stone lion suggests
the passage of time, and approaching death. How?

5   Now look at the way colour is used in the whole first verse.
Don't forget that 'bright' and 'dark' relate to colour.

6   The first sentence of the second verse, from 'My friend dead'
(line 7) to 'weeping in the air' describe what has happened
and is happening now to the speaker in the poem. The description
of the mourner's faces, though, makes connections with the first
verse. Look for connections between each of the first three words
in line 10 ('stony, rain, weeping') with an image in the first verse.

7 Look again at the last sentence in the second verse, from 'The grave' to 'fall of flowers' (lines 9–12). The sorrowing tone of the first two verses is gathered together here.

- The tone could be described as deep. How does the poet make the reader hear the word 'deep'? Think about where it is in the line, and what comes immediately before it.

- The grave is 'deep as a well'. Why does the poet use this comparison? Think of the previous line, and what a well holds.

- Which words in line 11 have a deep sound, to match the deep tone? How is the deep sound created?

- What 'fall of flowers' is taking place, do you think? How does this connect with the first verse?

- Something that ends with a sense of things going down is known as a dying fall. How many instances of things going down can you find in this sentence?

8 The pace of the third verse is much faster than the previous two. Line 12 is broken between the second and third verses. When the third verse begins, how do the words seem quicker? Think about the sound of the words, and alliteration (look back to Question 3).

9 Line 13 conveys speed in several ways.

- The first word is 'runs'. How is the idea of speed emphasised here by its position in the line, and by what comes next?

- What do you think the poet means by 'the wind's white steps over grass'? Think about what long grass looks like when a strong wind passes over it. How might this look like words on a page?

- The sounds are much lighter and quicker here than in the second verse. Which sounds, exactly? Look for alliteration again. There's a vowel sound repeated in the line, too – when a vowel sound is repeated for effect, it is called assonance. Which word in the line has the same vowel sound as 'grass'? How is this sound different to the dominant vowel sounds in the second verse?

10 Why do you think 'health feels like pain' (line 14) to the speaker?

11 Look at the next sentence, from 'Then panic' (line 14) to 'faded green' (line 17).

- What do you think causes 'panic' in the speaker's mind?

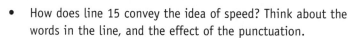

- How does line 15 convey the idea of speed? Think about the words in the line, and the effect of the punctuation.

- Time is linked to the passing of seasons throughout the poem. How is the movement of seasons suggested in this sentence? Think about the leaves and bushes, and the associations that come with the mention of a robin.

12 Now look at the last two lines of the poem.

- The speaker feels that she must write 'like the wind'. On one level, this simply means 'quickly'. But this is the third time wind has been mentioned in the poem. What else has it become associated with, apart from speed?

- What references are there to the passing of time in these lines?

- What do you think a 'death-day' is? The speaker hopes to pass her death-day – get ahead of it, maybe. Is this possible? Think about the panic she feels again.

- 'Winning ground' means getting ahead in the race, perhaps – but something else as well. Think about any other meanings of ground in this poem, and try to relate them to this line.

Final thoughts

The first verse provides the setting for the action, and the action occurs in the second verse. What is the third verse about?

Why do you think the speaker is driven to writing so quickly by her friend's death?

Why do you think the poem is called 'October'?

Comparisons

You could compare this poem with:

Seamus Heaney
- Mid-Term Break
- Storm on the Island

Pre-1914 Bank
- Tichborne's Elegy
- Inversnaid
- Ulysses

On the Train

Read and revise

The Paddington train crash occurred in October 1999. Thirty-one people were killed and 500 injured.

1 Look at the first line. How is being on the train like being 'cradled', do you think? There might be several meanings.

2 'Rocking, rocking the rails' (line 2).
- How does 'rocking' pick up an idea from the first line?
- Why is the word 'rocking' repeated? Think about the movement of the train. Look through the rest of the poem for more repetitions.

3 The personal stereo mentioned in lines 2 and 3 is a reminder that this is a recent poem, about communications. What other types of communication are mentioned in the poem?

4 Why does the tea 'tremble' (line 4)? What does this detail remind you of about the train?

5 Lines 5 and 6 are about two people thinking about each other. Why is this an important detail to put into the reader's mind at the beginning of the poem? Think about what happens later.

6 Look at the second verse.
- Why do you think such a wide range of places is mentioned in the first five lines of the verse?
- In lines 9–11, what sort of picture is drawn of the places that people travel from? Think about time of day, light, temperature and sound.
- The trains are 'dreaming their way' (line 12). How does this continue some of the ideas already established in the poem?
- The wrecked train is described as 'the blazing bone-ship'. How does this picture contrast with the scenes described in the rest of the verse?
- Vikings buried their heroes at sea, by sending them out in long boats which had been set alight. Why do you think the poet has made the reader think of this at this point? Think about appearance, and the emotional effect.

7 You probably recognise the sentence that forms the first two lines of the third verse (line 13–14). How has the poet made the sentence seem dramatic by making the line break after 'calling'?

8 Line 15 also begins with a familiar phrase, which is then used twice more in the next line and a half. Why do you think the poet has used these repetitions? Think about the number of calls, and why they are not answered.

9 'In the rubble' is repeated too, in lines 16 and 17, but the meaning of the phrase changes. What 'rubble' do you think might be in the 'suburban kitchens'? What has been wrecked here?

10 'Wolves howl' (line 18) compares the sound that wolves make to the voices of people in their kitchens. Why, do you think? Think about why the telephones are silent, and what this might mean.

11 Now look at the last verse, which brings the poem back to the voice and situation of the speaker, as it was at the end of the first verse.

- Why do you think the speaker is desperate to talk to her loved one? How does the poet show the desperation?

- In the context of what has happened at Paddington, why is 'I'll be home safe' (line 21) significant?

- 'Let them say it' (line 23). Who are the people the speaker is thinking of here? What would it mean if they were able to say 'I'm on the train'?

Final thoughts

Read the poem through again, thinking about the impact of the last line – 'Darling, I'm on the train'. What different meanings does 'on the train' have? How does the poet signal the importance of the phrase before the poem begins?

<table>
<tr><td rowspan="4">**Comparisons**</td><td colspan="2">**You could compare this poem with:**</td></tr>
<tr><td>**Seamus Heaney**</td><td>**Pre-1914 Bank**</td></tr>
<tr><td>• Mid-Term Break</td><td>• The Affliction of Margaret</td></tr>
<tr><td>• Storm on the Island</td><td>• The Little Boy Lost /
The Little Boy Found</td></tr>
</table>

Cold Knap Lake

Read and revise

Read the poem through once. When you've read to the end, you'll need to read it all again before attempting the questions below, because of the change in the poem at line 15.

1 Read the first stanza again (lines 1–4), which is the first stage of the event that happened.

- Two words in the first line tell you that this is an event that happened in the past, being remembered. Which words? How do they establish this as a past event?

- The poet plays several tricks with the reader's mind in this poem. When you first read the poem, how does line 2 convince you that the child is dead? How does line 4 hint that perhaps she isn't?

- Colours are significant in this poem, and the first two appear in line 3. What do you think the 'water's long green silk' that the child is 'dressed' in actually is? Think what might be at the bottom of the lake. The 'silk', though, contrasts with the child's real life. How?

2 Now read the second stanza, which describes the second stage of the event.

- What does the action of 'kneeling on the earth' (line 5) suggest? How does that suggestion connect with what the watching crowd might be thinking? Which phrase in line 6 continues the idea?

- How does the speaker's mother contrast with the drowned child? Think about colour, and how she is dressed.

- How does the mother seem alive, in contrast to the child?

- The mother is described as 'a heroine' in line 6. How does line 8 reinforce the idea of her being a heroine?

- The repetition of sounds connects things together. The 'crowd' are connected – the word means a number of people. How do the sounds in lines 9 and 10 connect, to match the idea? (Repetition of consonant sounds for effect is called alliteration.)

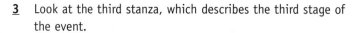

3 Look at the third stanza, which describes the third stage of the event.

- How do the watching crowd (and the reader) know that the child has been brought to life?

- Find the colour in this stanza. How has the child's colour changed? Why? Whose colour does it resemble now?

- 'A poor house' (line 13) suggests there is not much money in the house. Might 'poor' have any other meanings?

4 'Was I there?' (line 15) changes the poem.

- There is nothing in the first three stanzas to suggest that this is anything other than an accurate account of an event in the past. How does this line change that idea in the reader's minds?

- How does the poet let this moment register in the reader's mind? Think about the pause before the question, and look at the length of the line on the page, compared to the rest of the lines.

5 The question in line 15 raises uncertainty in the speaker's mind. Which other words in lines 16–18 suggest uncertainty? You should find at least four.

6 Lines 16–20 compare the lake, and what happened there, with the speaker's memory.

- How might the 'troubled surface' (line 16) refer to the lake and the mind?

- The branches of the willow are compared to 'dipped fingers'. How is this description true of the branches? How does it remind you of the child, even though the event might really be 'something else'?

- Which word in line 18 reminds you of the child in the water?

- The mud 'blooms' when it's disturbed by the swans as they leave. Which words in line 19 suggest how this has happened?

- The poet is comparing the way events become 'clouded' in the memory with the passing of time. If the swans represent the events, how does the poet suggest the movement of time? Look carefully at line 20, and think again about how the mud 'blooms in cloudiness'.

7 Now look at the last two lines, which stand on their own to complete the poem, drawing the two strands together.

- What are the 'lost things', do you think? How have they been lost?

- The water is described as 'closing'. If the water closes, what does it mean? Why has the poet chosen a word that suggests something that is happening now?

- Think about the word 'poor' again. What does it mean, do you think?

- Repetition of sounds connects things together. Here the child is connected with everything else in the speaker's mind. Which sound is repeated four times in these two lines (it's another alliteration). What do you notice about the last words in each of these lines? See if this device is used in the poem anywhere else.

Final thoughts

This appears to be a very simple poem, but in the end it isn't at all. Read the poem again, thinking about the connections between the lake and the memory.

Comparisons

You could compare this poem with:

Seamus Heaney
- Mid-Term Break
- Blackberry-Picking
- Follower
- Death of a Naturalist

Pre-1914 Bank
- On my first Sonne
- Tichborne's Elegy

Foundation Tier

1 Compare the ways that poets write about nature in **four or more** of the poems you have studied. You should write about **The Field-Mouse** by Gillian Clarke and **Storm on The Island** by Seamus Heaney, and **two poems** from the Pre-1914 Poetry Bank.

Remember to compare:

- what the poets write about
- the methods they use to write about nature.

2 **a** Compare the ways that Heaney writes about family relationships in **Mid-Term Break** and **Follower**.

   b Compare the ways that the writers of **two** of the poems in the Pre-1914 Poetry Bank write about family relationships.

Remember to write about:

- the relationships in the poems
- how the poets present the relationships.

Higher Tier

1 Compare the ways that poets use imagery in **four or more** of the poems you have studied. You should write about **October** by Gillian Clarke, and compare it with **one** poem by Seamus Heaney and **two** poems from the Pre-1914 Poetry Bank.

Remember to compare:

- the feelings the poets write about
- how they present feelings by the ways they write about them.

2 Seamus Heaney in **At a Potato Digging** and Walt Whitman in **Patrolling Barnegat** write very differently about nature, and use different poetic devices.

   a Compare these two poems

   b Compare them with **two** poems from the Pre-1914 Poetry Bank.

Carol Ann Duffy

a — Carol Ann Duffy was born in Glasgow in 1955. She has won many awards for poetry, including the Whitbread Poetry Award.

Havisham

g

Glossary

Miss Havisham is a character in *Great Expectations* by Charles Dickens. In the novel, she is an old woman who still wears her wedding dress. The rotting wedding cake is still on the table from the day the bridegroom did not appear many years before.

Read and revise

In this poem the poet creates the voice of a **persona** – a fictional character, though in this case a character created originally by someone else. Read the poem through once, registering the tone created by the character's words.

1 The sound of the words helps to create the character's feelings of anger and contempt. The frequent use of the sound created by the letter 'b' is particularly noticeable.

- Look at the first three words of the poem, noticing that 'b' begins the first and third word. How does this help to set the tone for the poem? Think what Miss Havisham's feelings are, and how you say the word 'bastard'. What sort of sound is 'b'? Think what your lips do when you say it – like spitting, almost.

- Now read from 'a red balloon' (line 13) to 'a wedding-cake' (line 14). Count the 'b' sounds here, including one inside a word. What sounds and feelings are they helping to convey here?

- 'B' ends the poem as well as beginning it. Look at the last word. How is 'b' used differently here?

2 The third word of the poem comes as a surprise, after the first two. Why? Are there any other indications in the poem that Miss Havisham feels anything else than hatred for the man who left her?

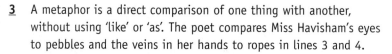

3 A metaphor is a direct comparison of one thing with another, without using 'like' or 'as'. The poet compares Miss Havisham's eyes to pebbles and the veins in her hands to ropes in lines 3 and 4.

- Why these things, do you think? How have prayer and time produced these effects?

- Why do you think the colour of the eyes is green?

- In what way has Miss Havisham become inhuman?

4 The combination of 'ropes' and 'strangle' is a violent image. What other words and phrases can you find in the poem that suggest violence or murder? These help to create the tone.

5 The first three words of the second verse also feature repeated sounds. Sounds connect things – why does Havisham connect the first and third word? The vowel sound is repeated, but so is the sound at the beginning of the words, nearly. What does this sound have in common with the 'b' at the beginning of the poem? Say it aloud again. Repetition of a consonant sound – like 'b' – for effect is known as alliteration.

6 The poet creates Miss Havisham's voice in several ways. How does she reflect the sound of the voice by 'Nooooo' in line 6? How does she repeat the same technique in the last line of the poem?

7 The poet uses sight as well as sound. The dress is 'yellowing' from white with the effect of time. Why do you think it is 'trembling' (line 7) in the mirror? Think about the person in it. The mirror is 'slewed' – how does this reflect Miss Havisham's view of things?

8 Miss Havisham seems uncertain of the identity of the person she sees in the mirror – 'her' and 'myself' are placed together on the line by the poet, who then adds 'who' to underline the effect. Why is this effect of uncertainty created, do you think? Why might she not recognise herself?

9 'Who did this / to me?' (lines 8–9) is split between two verses. What effect does the pause have when you read the lines? What does Miss Havisham mean?

10 Miss Havisham's curses are 'sounds not words' (line 9). How has the poet shown this in the poem?

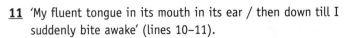

11 'My fluent tongue in its mouth in its ear / then down till I suddenly bite awake' (lines 10–11).

- Miss Havisham's tongue is certainly 'fluent' – find all the references to the words and sounds she uses in the poem. But these lines are also **ambiguous**. Ambiguous means a word or phrase having at least two interpretations.

- Why do you think the poet has not used commas to divide the list in this sentence? Think about pace, and what Miss Havisham might be feeling here – when she's asleep.

- There is a pause in the list, though, created by the line break. Why has the poet broken the line at this point? Think about the expectation created, and what comes after the break.

- When Miss Havisham 'bites awake' it is typical of her presentation in the rest of the poem – but what is she biting on here, exactly? Why might she want to do this?

- Why would Miss Havisham have this dream at all?

12 'Love's / hate behind a white veil' (lines 12–13).

- The apostrophe after 'love' is ambiguous (see Question 11). Work out both meanings, depending on what the apostrophe means.

- How does each meaning affect how you read 'behind a white veil'? What is the effect of the pause created by the verse break?

13 How might love be like 'a red balloon' (line 13)? Think what associations there are with balloons. Why red? How has the balloon burst in Miss Havisham's face?

14 'Bang' (line 14) is yet another sound in the poem, and it also creates an effect when the sounds in the word appear in the next sentence. You've already seen the consonant sound – but what about the vowel sound? Repeating a vowel sound to create an effect is called assonance.

15 Why do you think that Miss Havisham 'stabbed' at a wedding-cake? Notice the past tense – this was on the wedding day, presumably. What might she have expected to do to the cake?

16 Line 15 suggests several things. Why does she want 'a male corpse'? How has Miss Havisham's life been 'a long slow honeymoon'? Putting the two things together, what would Miss Havisham like to do with this male on a honeymoon? If you find this strange, think about Miss Havisham's state of mind.

17 Look at the last line of the poem. What else has been broken, apart from Miss Havisham's heart? What sound is the poet creating by repeating the 'b' in 'b-b-b-breaks'?

Final thoughts

If you haven't done so already, read the poem aloud – in your head if nothing else. Listen to the way the sounds and lines create Miss Havisham's voice.

Comparisons

You could compare this poem with:

Simon Armitage
- Kid
- 'Those bastards in their mansions'
- 'I've made out a will; I'm leaving myself'
- Hitcher
- November

Pre-1914 Bank
- The Song of the Old Mother
- The Laboratory
- The Affliction of Margaret

Elvis's Twin Sister

g

Glossary

Are you lonesome tonight?	title of an Elvis hit
Gregorian chant	ritual chant sung by Benedictines in the Catholic Church
pascha nostrum immolatus est	Latin for 'At Easter Christ (the lamb) was sacrificed for us'. Used as an Easter processional hymn
wimple	head covering worn by nuns
rosary	string of prayer beads
Blue suede shoes	title of an Elvis hit
Graceland	Elvis's mansion
Heartbreak Hotel	title of an Elvis hit. The last three lines of the poem echo the song directly

Read and revise

This poem is full of fun – the idea is humorous, and the poet plays with words and ideas throughout. Since the death of Elvis in 1977, many people have claimed to see him alive in all sorts of peculiar places. Read the poem through once, noticing some of the ways the poet joins Elvis with this unlikely setting.

<u>1</u> Look at the two **epigraphs**. An epigraph is a quotation at the beginning of a piece of writing, which might suggest its theme.

- The first quotation reminds you that Elvis's fans missed him after his death – perhaps the reason for all the sightings. But what does the second quotation suggest? Who is the person in the convent, perhaps?

- Notice who the second quotation is from, too. How is this person particularly apt to quote in this poem? Think about the associations with her name.

<u>2</u> Why is Elvis appearing as a nun funny in itself? Apart from the idea of cross-dressing for such a male figure as Elvis, you could research some of the reasons for Elvis causing such outrage (and attraction) when he first became famous.

<u>3</u> Look at the first verse (lines 1–5). In this verse the poet begins to create the voice of the persona in the poem. A persona is a fictional character, though here it is a real one, perhaps – unless it really is an imagined twin sister!

- Look at the language of the verse. Which phrase (apart from 'rock 'n' roll') stands out as being different to the rest? How does this rather odd joining of two types of language reflect the whole situation?

- In the lyrics of 'American Pie', these words appear: 'Do you believe in rock and roll? / Can music save your mortal soul?' How do lines 4 and 5 play on the joining together of God and rock and roll? Which phrase does it?

- There isn't a regular rhyme scheme in the poem, but rhymes keep appearing – as though Elvis (or his sister) can't help singing. Where is the first rhyme in the poem?

<u>4</u> Look at the second verse (lines 6–10).

- Like the first verse, there's one line that doesn't fit with the religious setting. Which is it? How do both the language and the idea seem funny, given the place and the person described?

- How is 'Sister Presley' a play on words? Remember who she is – perhaps.

- The word 'digs' has two meanings, of course, which the poet is playing with. What do the women in the convent seem to do, judging by the first verse?

- 'Brother' is literal – just like Elvis, she means. But what does 'Brother' also mean, in the context of this place?

- Where is the rhyme here?

5 How does the music mentioned at the beginning of the third verse contrast with what Elvis (or his sister) might be expected to enjoy?

6 The sacrificed lamb, 'Pascha nostrum', (line 13) might have one meaning for the nuns, but another for the speaker. Can you connect the phrase with the previous line? If the Latin phrase makes the reader think of Easter, are there any other meanings possible for Elvis?

7 Look at the description of how Elvis (or his sister) is dressed, from 'I wear a simple habit' (line 14) to 'blue suede shoes' (line 20). The list is quite long, and all of the items fit the context of a convent – until the last one. Why do you think the poet holds this detail back until the end? How is the change underlined by the preceding line? How is it underlined by rhyme, so that it seems a natural conclusion, when actually it's not? Why is the detail funny?

8 Look again at the fifth verse (lines 21–25).

- How does the speaker join the convent and Elvis's home by playing with words? Why does the thought make Elvis (or his sister) smile, do you think?

- The word 'back' in line 25 is the biggest hint so far that this might be Elvis himself. How?

- Where is the rhyme in this verse?

9 Look at the last verse, which is full of echoes of Elvis.

- 'Lawdy' is an expression of surprise, of course, written in a Southern States accent. It's also a reminder, perhaps, of 'Lawdy Miss Clawdy', another Elvis number. But it's a play on words, as well. What does it actually mean, and refer to?

- 'I'm alive and well' is another hint about the identity of the speaker. How? It's also the beginning of a common expression – 'He's alive and well and living in . . . '. How does this thought fit the poem, and what the speaker is saying and feeling in this verse?

• 'Heartbreak Hotel' was Elvis's first big hit, which is why it's a 'Long time', perhaps. There's something else, though. Where might 'Heartbreak Hotel' and 'Lonely Street' have been in Elvis's past life? Think about the previous verse again.

Final thoughts

Read the poem again. Does the speaker seem to enjoy his / her life in the convent? Why, do you think? Find all the evidence you can.

Comparisons

You could compare this poem with:

Simon Armitage
• Kid
• 'Those bastards in their mansions'
• 'I've made out a will; I'm leaving myself'
• Hitcher
• November

Pre-1914 Bank
• The Song of the Old Mother
• Sonnet 130
• Ulysses

Anne Hathaway

g

Glossary

Anne Hathaway	William Shakespeare's wife. She married him in 1582, when she was 18. She died in 1623. Shakespeare died in 1616.
assonance	the repetition of vowel sounds to create an effect in writing

Read and revise

Shakespeare's sonnets were about love, and often about writing too. Read this poem through once to start to see how this poem combines both of these elements as well. The poet creates the persona of Anne Hathaway in this poem, the voice of her character – but the voice is close to Shakespeare's voice, too.

1 The poet chooses to write a **sonnet** to echo Shakespeare. Shakespeare's sonnets were of fourteen lines with a regular rhyme scheme, as you can see if you look at **Sonnet 130** on page 50 of

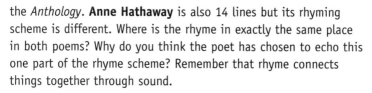

the *Anthology*. **Anne Hathaway** is also 14 lines but its rhyming scheme is different. Where is the rhyme in exactly the same place in both poems? Why do you think the poet has chosen to echo this one part of the rhyme scheme? Remember that rhyme connects things together through sound.

<u>2</u> The poet uses another feature of Shakespeare's writing – the **iambic pentameter**. This describes a line of poetry with ten syllables. There are five beats in the line, the stress falling on the second syllable of each pair. The line can then be varied for effect. Look at any of the first three lines of this poem, counting syllables and beats, and noticing where the stresses fall. These are regular iambic pentameters. If you look at **Sonnet 130**, you'll see the same thing there.

<u>3</u> Shakespeare's writing was full of **imagery** – all sorts of comparisons, used to make the reader understand what he was describing.

- What is the bed compared to in the first line of the poem? How does the poet then develop the metaphor in lines 2 and 3? A metaphor is a direct comparison between one thing and another, without using 'like' or 'as'.

- How do you think the bed might have been like 'a spinning world'? If you know any of Shakespeare's plays, you'll probably recognise some of the places in line 2.

- Notice where the last stress of line 1 falls – on which word? Why does the poet choose to emphasise this word, do you think? Think about the word itself, and what comes after it.

<u>4</u> What are Shakespeare's words compared to in line 4? How does this poet develop the metaphor? Notice that the last stress of the line falls on 'kisses', and there's a line break after it – which word does the pause make you linger over? How does that fit the feelings of Anne Hathaway in the poem?

<u>5</u> Look at the three lines from 'my body now' (line 5) to 'the centre of a noun' (line 7), where the poet compares love to language.

- Pick out all the words that refer to language in these lines. How are these suitable words to use in a poem about Shakespeare as a lover?

- The poet compares the relationship of her body to his as 'rhyme', 'echo', and 'assonance'. Why these things? Think what all of these words mean, in terms of words, which might be applied to the couple in the bed.

- How do you think his touch might be 'a verb dancing in the centre of a noun'? Think again about the words themselves – what sort of words do they describe, which might be compared to this situation?

6 Look at the sentence beginning 'Some nights' (lines 8–9).

- What is the bed compared to? Why? What is the effect of the line break after 'bed'?

- You're reading a piece of writing here. Work out exactly what's going on in the line. You could start: 'The poet imagines (in writing) a woman dreaming that a poet has imagined (in writing) that ...'!

7 'Romance / and drama' (lines 9–10) describe what happened in the bed. Why does the poet use these words to describe it? The word 'played' helps. They are played by 'touch, by scent, by taste'. Why these things? Think about writing as well as loving.

8 Look at the sentence beginning 'In the other bed' (lines 11–12).

- Although lines 11 and 12 don't rhyme, in the sense that the two words at the end don't rhyme, there are two pairs of words within this sentence that do rhyme. Find them, and work out why the poet has chosen rhyming words for each pair – what connections are being made by sound?

- The guests are 'dribbling their prose'. How does this contrast with the couple in the 'second best bed', do you think?

9 'My living laughing love' (line 12) clearly demonstrates alliteration – the repetition of consonant sounds (the 'l' here) for effect. What things are being drawn together? Think about each of these words in connection with Anne Hathaway's dead husband, Shakespeare.

10 Look at the last two lines of the poem.

- What does the speaker compare her head to in line 13? Why is it appropriate? Picture it as well as thinking about the idea.

- She holds him 'as he held me'. If she means that exactly, how does it add to the picture in her head?

- The last two lines rhyme. Partly, this echoes Shakespeare's own sonnets, but there's another reason. What two things are connected strongly by the rhyme? Where has all of this poem 'happened'?

Final thoughts

This poem is full of cleverly-used devices, as is fitting for a poem about Shakespeare that uses some of his techniques. It's more than that, though. Read the poem again, concentrating on Anne Hathaway's feelings.

One of Shakespeare's best known sonnets 'Shall I compare thee to a summer's day?' is about love, and about writing too, like this poem. It ends:

'So long as men can breathe, or eyes can see,
So long lives this, and this gives life to thee.'

How has Carol Ann Duffy 'given life' to Anne Hathaway in this poem?

Comparisons

You could compare this poem with:

Simon Armitage
- Kid
- 'Those bastards in their mansions'
- 'Mother, any distance greater than a single span'

Pre-1914 Bank
- Sonnet 130
- Sonnet (Clare)
- My Last Duchess

Salome

Glossary

In Christian history, Salome was the daughter of Herodias and the stepdaughter of Herod Antipas. Herodias wanted St John the Baptist killed because he had condemned her marriage. She persuaded Salome to 'seduce' Herod with a dance, then make him promise to give her whatever she wished. Salome asked for the head of St John the Baptist on a platter, which Herod had to agree to. Salome brought it to her mother. In Strauss's opera *Salome*, based on Oscar Wilde's play about her, Salome desires John, but the only way she can have a part of him is to have the head, as he has rejected her. She kisses the lips of his decapitated head.

Read and revise

In this poem Carol Ann Duffy creates a persona – the voice of a fictional character. Here, though, the poet gives the biblical character's voice a very modern feel, to make the character 'come alive'. Read the poem through once, following the story and noticing how modern the voice seems.

1 One noticeable feature of Salome's voice is her 'patter' – the way her language swings along. This is partly created by a feature that runs right through the poem.

- Look at the last words in line 3, line 7 and line 9 – 'later', 'lighter', 'laughter'. The sound of these three words is nearly the same, because the same consonants are used, and only the vowels change. This is called consonant rhyme or **half-rhyme**. There are other half-rhymes in the poem, and words which just echo some sounds – 'later' and 'matter', for instance, make similar sounds. Work right through the poem, picking out all the half-rhymes and echoes you can – you'll see there are a lot.

- The final echo comes on the last word – 'platter'. There are so many 'ter' words, it's as though the whole poem is aimed at this last word. Why has the poet chosen to do this, do you think? Think about Salome's story in the poem, and the most famous feature of the Bible story.

2 Salome's language is clearly modern, not biblical.

- There are several words and phrases that belong to modern slang – they're colloquial. Find as many as you can. You could begin with 'a night on the batter' (line 23).

- The voice created is casual, as though she's talking to you – gossiping, perhaps. 'Like I said' (line 35), for instance, is clearly conversational. Can you find any other words and phrases (apart from those you've already found) that belong to a conversation, rather than writing?

3 What sort of person is the Salome that the poet has created? Look for her attitudes and feelings, and find evidence in the poem for your conclusions. For instance, what do 'doubtless I'll do it again' (line 2) and 'whose? – what did it matter?' (lines 4–5) tell you about her?

4 When you first read the poem, what does 'a head on the pillow beside me' (line 4) seem to mean? In retrospect, why might the hair be 'rather matted' (line 6) and the beard 'reddish' (line 7)? Why might the deep lines round the eyes be 'from pain'?

5 Why is the man's mouth 'colder than pewter' (line 13), actually? The comparison isn't casual – what might be made from pewter?

6 Look at the list of four names in lines 14 and 15.

- What does it tell you about Salome that she can't remember the man's name?

- Why has the poet created a large gap between the first two names in the list, do you think, and why has she placed the real name last in the list?

- Why has the poet chosen these particular names? What do they remind the reader about?

7 Look at the two lines 'Her clearing of clutter / her regional patter' (lines 20–21).

- 'Clutter' and 'patter' echo with each other, and form half-rhymes with words elsewhere. There are more sound repetitions in the poem, though, to add to the swing of the language. Which sound is repeated in line 20? Repetition of consonant sounds for effect is called alliteration.

- The 'swing' is created by rhythm, too. Say these two lines aloud. How does the rhythm of the two lines sound similar? Work out where the beats come to make it like this. Can you find any other lines in the poem with the same rhythm?

8 'Wrecked' (line 23) has a modern colloquial meaning, but it has a literal meaning too. 'Wrecked' is rather ironic here. Who else is 'wrecked', apart from Salome?

9 Look at lines 29 and 30. There are three words which rhyme, or half-rhyme here. Which?

10 Salome refers to the body as coming 'like a lamb to the slaughter / to Salome's bed' (lines 31–32).

- What does she mean by this, do you think? What does it reveal about her?

- How is the phrase ironic? Think about the difference between what she means, and what has actually happened.

- The phrase also reminds the reader about the context of the story. Find out where it comes from.

11 Why do you think Salome's eyes 'glitter' (line 33)?

12 'Ain't life a bitch' (line 35), like 'a lamb to the slaughter' is a common phrase, but the poet has uses it cleverly. What does she actually see? What might the reader think of her?

Final thoughts

Part of the fun of this poem is that this Salome can't remember the night before, when it must have been quite dramatic, to say the least. Why can't she remember? What other fun is there in the poem?

Comparisons

You could compare this poem with:

Simon Armitage	Pre-1914 Bank
• Kid	• The Laboratory
• 'Those bastards in their mansions'	• The Affliction of Margaret
• Hitcher	• Ulysses

Before You Were Mine

g

Glossary

Marilyn	There is a famous photograph of Marilyn Monroe holding her dress down as the wind from a ventilation shaft in the pavement blows it up.
George Square, Portobello	places in Glasgow

Read and revise

This is a poem about the poet's relationship with her mother, even before she was born. Read the poem through once, thinking about the mother's character and how the poet feels about her.

1 The most interesting – and complicated – feature of this poem is the way the poet uses time. It's important to work out the different times referred to in the poem.

- The first two verses are both set at the same time. When was this? The best clues are in the first line, and the first line of the third verse.

- What happened ten years after the time that the first two verses are set in?

- Line 12 is set in a different time. How old do you think the speaker might have been when she put 'my hands in those high-heeled red shoes'?

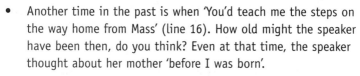

- Another time in the past is when 'You'd teach me the steps on the way home from Mass' (line 16). How old might the speaker have been then, do you think? Even at that time, the speaker thought about her mother 'before I was born'.

- The final time is 'now' (line 13). Where is the speaker when she imagines her mother 'under the tree'?

2 The title of the poem refers to time too, and does something else.

- The word 'Before' suggests that the focus of the poem will be one of the times you have identified in Question 1. Which one?

- Who is the 'you' in the title? 'You Were Mine' suggests possession. How is this possession a reversal of what you might usually expect between mother and child?

3 In the first line, the poet plays with the idea of distance and time. Being 'ten years away from the corner' is a surprising idea – why? What does the poet actually mean?

4 In the first verse there is a strong sense of life being enjoyed. Which words and ideas suggest this?

5 Look at verse 2 (lines 6–10).

- Why is the speaker 'not here yet' (line 6)? Why doesn't 'the thought of me' occur in the ballroom?

- What was the mother thinking about in the ballroom, do you think? Find evidence. What would 'the right walk home' mean?

- Why does the mother behave like this 'before you were mine'?

- 'Before you were mine, your Ma stands ...' (line 9) gives a sense of continuity of time and relationships. How?

- What does 'You reckon it's worth it' suggest about the mother? Think about line 11. What do you think the speaker's attitude to her mother is?

6 Which words in line 11 suggest reasons for the best years of the mother's life being the decade before the child was born? Think about the enjoyment shown in the second verse.

7 Which 'high-heeled red shoes' might the child be thinking of? What are they 'relics' of? What does the word 'relics' suggest about the mother's life with the child, and her life before the child was born?

8 Ghosts don't usually 'clatter'. Why does this ghost 'clatter'? Think about Question 7. Is this a 'real' ghost? What is the poet describing, exactly?

9 Lines 13–15 use sight, smell and touch to conjure up the 'ghost'.

- 'Clear as scent' is an unusual simile. A simile is a comparison of one thing with another, without using 'like' or 'as'. What does 'scent' suggest about this ghost? Why?

- Look at 'Lights' and 'bites' in line 15 rhyme. Why are these two things connected through sound? Think about 'I see you' (line 14).

- What does line 15 suggest about the speaker's mother? What is the speaker's attitude to her mother here? Now do you know?

10 What does 'stamping stars' (line 17) suggest about the mother's vigour? What do this and '*Cha cha cha!*' (line 16) suggest about the child's attitude to the mother?

11 Why was this 'the wrong pavement', do you think? You could think about 'the right walk home' (line 8).

12 Look carefully at the last three lines of the poem.

- Find all the evidence you can of the mother's character, and the child's attitude to her.

- What is the effect of the list of verbs in the last line? Notice that they are separated by using 'and'.

- Who is the 'love' for? It 'lasts' between which times that are mentioned in the poem? It might help to look back to Question 1.

Final thoughts

Read the poem again, thinking about what the woman was like when she was young, and when the child was young. How does the child feel about her mother? Finally, you might think about the title again – 'Before You Were Mine'.

Comparisons

You could compare this poem with:

Simon Armitage
- Homecoming
- 'Mother, any distance greater than a single span'
- 'My father thought it ...'

Pre-1914 Bank
- On my first Sonne
- The Affliction of Margaret
- The Song of the Old Mother

We Remember Your Childhood Well

> **Glossary**
>
> **the bad man on**   the Lancashire moors were the site of several
> **the moors**   grisly child murders in the 1960s.
>
> **Film Fun**   a monthly magazine about films

Read and revise

Read the poem through once. This is an adult voice (or voices) – is it telling the truth, do you think? Has the poet created a voice that is comforting, reassuring, threatening – how does it seem to you?

1   The voice the poet has created has a strong sense of control, partly created by the sentence forms she has chosen.

- Look at all the sentences in the poem. Are they commands, statements or questions?

- You'll have seen that there is only one question. What sort of question is it? How would the child being spoken to feel when they heard this question?

2   The form of the poem creates one half of a dialogue. You know what the adult voice says, but you have to guess at the other half of it. Although the older voice doesn't ask questions, the younger voice that you don't hear clearly is asking questions.

- Which of the statements are answers to questions, do you think?

- Which statements are denials of something? Count the number of times 'Nobody' and 'no' are used.

- Do so many denials make you suspicious?

3   The statements and commands create a sense of certainty – the voice is certain of what it says. Some other features of the writing add to this effect.

- The poem does not rhyme regularly, but there are some rhymes (not always entirely at the end of lines) to create a voice in tune with itself. What rhymes can you find?

- There is very little **imagery** in this poem – similes or metaphors, for instance. Why not, do you think? Part of line 10 might help you decide.

4 Whose is the voice that the poet has created, do you think? Is it one person, or two? What single voice might still use the term 'we' to describe itself?

5 The first verse is mostly denials of common childhood fears and problems, so that the reader might think that the child really did imagine things. What are the common fears or difficulties that are mentioned? What 'natural' explanation is given for one of them?

6 Look at the second verse (lines 4–6), which introduces a new element.

- What seems unlikely about 'Your questions were answered fully'? Think about the age of the child when these events did, or didn't, take place.

- The rest of the verse seems to be a denial that a particular event took place. The reader doesn't know what it is, of course, because the question isn't heard. Does it matter? Think what the whole poem is about.

- 'No. That didn't occur' is very definite. Is there any indication in the rest of the verse that the memory is not at all as clear as the speaker suggests? This would suggest that the speaker is lying, wouldn't it?

- 'Film Fun' and the 'coal fire' suggest things from the past. Why do you think the poet chooses to compare the sound of the magazine burning to 'laughing itself to death'? The speaker might be just conveying the blur of the past – but what is the effect on the reader's perception of the speaker?

7 Look at verse three (lines 7–9), where the speaker tries to convince the grown-up child about the past.

- What 'evidence' does the speaker have to support the opening statement, 'Nobody forced you'?

- What does the speaker mean by the statement 'The whole thing is inside your head'? All memories are inside the head, though. What effect may this childhood have had on the child? Why is it 'inside your head', in a different sense – and maybe true in a different way?

8 Look at verse four (lines 10–12).

- Which words in the verse suggest control and command? Which suggest that the child was inferior?

- Why do you think the older people are compared to 'secret police'?

- The sound of the voices is conveyed by 'Boom. Boom. Boom.'
  The poet is using onomatopoeia – the sound of the words
  matches the sound of the thing itself. Why will these sorts of
  voices have sounded like 'Boom. Boom. Boom.'? Think about
  the feeling of this verse.

9 Verse five looks like another past event being questioned, and
denied. What was the child's view of this event, and the people
involved? What sounds like excuses to you? What do you know
happened to the child? Notice there's a rhyme again.

10 Look at the last verse (lines 16–18).

- Why do you think 'no' is repeated in line 16? Think about what
  the older child might have said, and what being so insistent
  might suggest about the speaker.

- The child is clearly blaming the adults for the 'skidmarks of sin'
  on their soul, and being left 'wide open for Hell'. What do you
  think this means? At the very least, what does the child think
  its childhood has done to it?

- 'You were loved.' Is there any reason in the rest of the poem to
  doubt this? Why do you think the poet introduces this idea
  right at the end? Are you more or less likely to believe it here,
  than if it was said earlier?

- In the context of the whole poem, what does 'We did what was
  best' mean? What does 'We remember your childhood well' mean?

Final thoughts

The first sentence of the poem is 'Nobody hurt you.' Is this true?
What do you think might have happened to the child? If the child
was hurt, was it intentional? Does the speaker know if the child
was hurt or not?

What do you think this poem is about, in the end?

Comparisons

You could compare this poem with:

Simon Armitage

- Homecoming
- Kid
- 'Mother, any distance greater
  than a single span'
- 'My father thought it ...'

Pre-1914 Bank

- The Little Boy Lost /
  The Little Boy Found
- The Laboratory
- The Affliction of Margaret
- On my first Sonne

Education for Leisure

Read and revise

This poem creates a persona – the voice of a fictional character. Read the poem through once, trying to decide what sort of person this is.

1 The person in the poem is violent. Find as many violent actions, thoughts or intentions as you can in the poem.

2 The person is also vain. Find as many examples as you can of the person being vain.

3 The poet creates a striking voice in the poem, by choosing words and sentences carefully.

4 The words are all fairly simple, but the sentence forms are too. Many begin with the subject and verb, as in 'I am going to play God' (line 3). Although this is quite usual, if a lot of sentences are like this it becomes a very noticeable feature, and makes you think about the nature of the speaker. How many of the sentences here are simple sentences? What does it make you think about the speaker? Remember the title, too.

5 There is very little imagery in this poem – apart from verse two. Otherwise, there really isn't any. The language is very plain, and factual. What does this make you think of the speaker?

6 Look at the first verse (lines 1–4).

   • What is the effect of the first line, when you first read the poem? What does 'Anything' (with a full stop after it) add to the effect?

   • The second line suggests a reason for the behaviour of the speaker. What other reasons are suggested in the poem? There's another one in this verse, and others hinted at elsewhere.

   • 'I am going to play God'. What does the speaker do in the poem that is like 'playing God'?

7 Look at the second verse (lines 5–8).

   • Why do you think the poet has included the first sentence here? Notice that it is an end-stopped line – there's a full stop at the end of it. What is the effect of this?

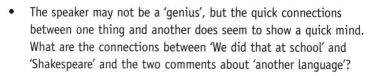

- The speaker may not be a 'genius', but the quick connections between one thing and another does seem to show a quick mind. What are the connections between 'We did that at school' and 'Shakespeare' and the two comments about 'another language'?

- 'The fly is in another language' (line 7). What language has the fly been translated into?

- What is the 'talent' that the speaker breathes out? What does this make you think about the speaker?

8 There's another quick shift of thought in the third verse, from 'I am going to change the world' to 'Something's world' (lines 10–11). How is the speaker going to change 'something's world'?

9 Look at the first two lines of verse four (lines 13–15). Do you think that these two lines are humorous? How? Notice the form and length of the sentences here.

10 Is the speaker serious about the autograph not being appreciated (line 16), do you think? What does the comment show about the speaker?

11 What is the connection between 'He cuts me off' (line 19), and 'I get our bread-knife'? Think about why the speaker does this at this moment, and the connection in language.

12 Why do you think that the pavements 'glitter suddenly'? Think about what the poet might be reflecting about the speaker's mind. Does the phrase connect with anything?

13 'I touch your arm' clearly creates a sense of threat. How? Think about:

- the opening of the poem
- the character of the speaker
- the fact that this is a short sentence, and the last one
- 'your arm' mentions the arm specifically, and 'your' for the first time.

Final thoughts

Think about the title. 'Education for Leisure' is one of the aims of school education. What has it meant for this person? What does the speaker do now? What is 'leisure' here? Read the poem again.

You could compare this poem with:

Simon Armitage

- Homecoming
- Kid
- Hitcher

Pre-1914 Bank

- The Little Boy Lost /
  The Little Boy Found
- The Laboratory
- My Last Duchess
- The Man He Killed

Stealing

Read and revise

This poem creates a persona – the voice of a fictional character. Read the poem through once, trying to decide what sort of person this is.

<u>1</u> The poet writes as if the speaker is trying to explain his or her actions – like a confession, almost. What drives the speaker? What does the speaker think of himself (or herself)? What do you think the gender of this person is? 'The slice of ice / within my own brain' suggests that the mind is cold. What else can you find in the poem which reveals what the speaker thinks?

<u>2</u> How does the first line suggest that this is part of a conversation?

<u>3</u> In the first verse, the speaker sees a connection between the snowman and himself, or herself.

- What similarity is there? Think about what the speaker says, and the snowman being 'a mute' (line 2). How might the speaker be a mute?

- The poet matches the connection between the speaker and the snowman with connections between the sounds of the words used to describe them. Count the number of 'm' and 'n' sounds in lines 1–4, beginning with 'snowman'. Which two words at the ends of lines form a **half-rhyme**, where the consonants rhyme but the vowel changes? Which words in line 4 rhyme?

- The poet makes a connection between the snowman and the speaker in a different way in line 5. What is it?

<u>4</u> Another link between the snowman and the speaker is made by a rhyme in line 5, at the end of the first verse, and the sound of a word in the first line of the second verse, line 6. Find it.

5 How does the connection between the speaker and the snowman become physical in the second verse? What is the effect of the physical closeness on the speaker?

6 'Chill' at the end of line 8 and 'thrill' in line 9 rhyme. What is being connected with the speaker's feelings, through the rhyming words?

7 What is revealed about the speaker by the 'thrill' (line 9)?

8 'Life's tough' (line 10). How does this reveal the speaker's attitude? Think about:

- what it means
- the sound of the words
- the length of the sentence
- where it appears in the line, and the verse
- the full stop after it, at the end of the line.

9 Look at the third verse (lines 11–15).

- The first, second and fourth verses are about stealing the snowman. What is the purpose of the third verse, do you think?
- How do the speaker's actions seem to be without purpose in this verse?
- The speaker sees himself, 'or herself', as a watcher, in this verse, almost outside the actions being performed. Find as many examples of this as you can. Why are 'mirrors' mentioned?
- Why do you think the sigh is mentioned? Think about what the speaker might be doing, and think about the form of this speech, too. What sort of sound is the '*Aah*', do you think?

10 Why is the word 'Again' (line 18) repeated, do you think? What is the speaker (and the poet) conveying? How else is violence conveyed by the poet's choice of words in lines 18 and 19?

11 What is the effect of the action on the speaker?

12 In the fourth verse, how are you reminded that the speaker is thinking about something in the past?

13 Now look at the last verse (lines 21–25).

- What reason does the speaker suggest for these actions in this verse?
- What sort of things are the guitar and the bust of Shakespeare? What might it suggest that the speaker was going to do, which is then denied?

- The last line reminds you of what sort of communication this seems to be – look back to the first line. 'You' appears for the first time in this last line, though – the person being addressed. Who do you think 'you' is?

- 'You don't understand a word I'm saying'. Why would 'you' not understand, do you think? Think again about who 'you' might be, and the speaker's view of himself, or herself.

Final thoughts

Now you've worked through the poem, think again about the character of the speaker, and the ways the poet has conveyed it, through the speaker's own voice. Has the 'stealing' really been fully explained? If not, maybe this is quite deliberate. Think about the last line again.

Comparisons

You could compare this poem with:

Simon Armitage
- Hitcher
- Kid

Pre-1914 Bank
- The Laboratory
- The Man He Killed
- Ulysses

Simon Armitage

a
Simon Armitage was born in West Yorkshire in 1963. In 1993 he was named The Sunday Times Young Writer of the Year. He works as a freelance writer and broadcaster.

'Mother, any distance greater than a single span'

g

Glossary

* This poem is from *Book of Matches*. The title of each poem is an asterisk, meant to represent the flame of a match in a party game. Somebody has to strike a match, then tell the story of their lives before the flame burns their fingers.

Read and revise

This poem is about time and distance between a mother and son – how they get farther apart as the boy grows, and leaves home, but remain joined too. The act of measuring rooms and windows in a new house symbolises this. Read the poem through once, to get the shape of it.

1 The distance between mother and son grows as the son moves through the house, further away from his mother, holding the end of the measuring tape. Find all the references to different parts of the house in the poem, and all the references to distances. There is only one specific reference to time. Find it.

2 A sonnet is a poem with fourteen lines, with a regular rhyme scheme. The poet plays with sonnet form here – this is almost a sonnet, but not quite.

* Which lines rhyme?

* Why do you think the poet has chosen to rhyme words at the beginning of the poem, then not again until the end? Rhyme connects things – think about the movement in the poem.

* 'Sky / fly' forms a sort of **rhyming couplet** at the end, but it doesn't quite fit the sonnet form – 'to fall or fly' is on the fifteenth line, and it's short. Why do you think the poet chooses to do this? Is the connection between mother and son here, or not?

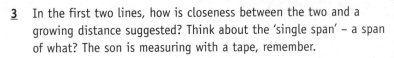

<u>3</u>   In the first two lines, how is closeness between the two and a growing distance suggested? Think about the 'single span' – a span of what? The son is measuring with a tape, remember.

<u>4</u>   Lines 3 and 4 state clearly what is happening in the poem. Why are the walls described as 'acres', and the floors 'prairies', do you think? Think about shape and size, and the distance between the two people. A metaphor is the term for a direct comparison, which doesn't use 'like' or 'as'.

<u>5</u>   The mother is at the 'zero-end' (line 5) literally, holding the end of the tape. She's at the zero-end metaphorically, too – the zero-end of the relationship between mother and son. How? Think about how the relationship started.

<u>6</u>   As the distance between mother and son grows – as he gets older – he reports 'back to base' (line 6). How is the mother the 'base', both in measuring the house, and in the boy's life?

<u>7</u>   Bearing in mind what is being described in the poem, why do you think the poet chooses to break the phrase 'leaving / up the stairs' (lines 6–7) with a line break after the word 'leaving'? Think about the effect as you read it, and which word you linger over.

<u>8</u>   The idea of the distance between them as they measure the house being like the distance in time as the boy grows older is made explicit in lines 7 and 8. How?

<u>9</u>   'Anchor. Kite' (line 8) introduces two more metaphors for the relationship between mother and son.

- Like the measuring tape, the anchor brings to mind two things joined by something stretched between them. Which is trying to move? How is the mother like an 'anchor', do you think?

- 'Kite' brings to mind two more things joined by something stretched between them. Which is holding something in place? How is the son like a 'kite', do you think?

<u>10</u> Why do you think the bedrooms are 'empty'? Think about two houses – the one the son is leaving, and the one he's going to.

<u>11</u> 'Breaking point, where something / has to give' (lines 10–11) describes the tape between them being at full stretch. How might this also apply to the relationship between mother and son? Like 'leaving' in line 6, why has the poet broken the phrase 'something / has to give' with a line break?

12 How might lines 12 and 13 describe the mother's attitude to the son, as well as the way she holds on to the end of the tape?

13 The poet is playing with the verse form. How does he start to introduce rhyme at the end of the poem even before the last two lines? Say lines 12 and 13 aloud.

14 Look at the last sentence, from 'I reach' (line 13) to the end.

- Why does the poet break the phrase 'reach / towards a hatch' with a line break? Think about the word that's lingered over when you read it, and the gap created.

- What does the 'endless sky' represent, that the son is looking at when he opens the hatch?

- Why might he 'fall or fly', do you think? What is being described? What does this imply about the line between the mother and son?

- Why do you think the last phrase, 'to fall or fly', is separated, to form a line on its own? Think about the line between mother and son again.

Final thoughts

Read the poem again, noticing exactly how the poet has made the measuring of the house symbolise the distance between mother and son. What point in the relationship has been reached? What event in the son's life might the poem be describing?

You could compare this poem with:

Carol Ann Duffy
- Before You Were Mine
- We Remember Your Childhood Well

Pre–1914 Bank
- The Song of the Old Mother
- Sonnet 130
- The Little Boy Lost / The Little Boy Found

Comparisons

'My father thought it ...'

g

> **Glossary**
>
> * This poem is from *Book of Matches*. The title of each poem is an asterisk, meant to represent the flame of a match in a party game. Somebody has to strike a match, and then tell the story of their lives before the flame burns their fingers.

Read and revise

This is a fairly simple poem, on the surface. Read it through once, listening to the two voices in the poem – the father's and the son's. Whose voice does the last line of the poem (the one in italics) belong to, do you think?

1 A sonnet is a poem with fourteen lines, with a regular rhyme scheme. The poet plays with sonnet form here – this is almost a sonnet, but not quite.

   • Which lines rhyme?

   • This poem is fifteen lines long, not fourteen, so it's not a sonnet. Look at the end of the poem, though. If the poem ended before the italics start, what would the poem look like? Would it end on a rhyme? What does the italicised line become?

2 The poem is organised into three stanzas. Try to decide what each one is about, so that the breaks between stanzas reflect breaks in the thought in the poem.

3 Look at the first stanza (lines 1–5), which gives the father's attitude.

   • What are the father's attitudes to the ring and to his son in this verse?

   • What do the father's language, and his attitudes, reveal about him?

   • The rhyme in this verse is regular – everything is connected together by the rhymes. Why has the poet chosen to do this, do you think? Think what all of the verse is about.

4 The second stanza (lines 6–11) doesn't seem to rhyme in the same way as the first, but there are some echoes and rhymes nevertheless.

   • Which word rhymes with 'skin' (line 7)? It's not at the end of a line.

- What does 'sleeper' (line 10) connect with, in both sound and sense?

- Which words actually form a full rhyme?

5 The speaker says that he 'hadn't the nerve' (line 6). How is the speaker's lack of physical bravery shown several times in the second stanza?

6 How does the poet play with the word 'sleeper' (line 10)?

7 Line 12 introduces a change in the poem. What is the change in the time setting? Think about the tense of the verb in this line, then the tense of all the verbs up to this point in the poem.

8 Why do you think the speaker mentions that he is now 'twenty-nine'? How long ago might the earlier events have been?

9 Although the ear-piercing happens at some time in the past, the poet connects the two times cleverly, through the word 'wept' (line 11). What does 'wept' actually mean in line 11? How does the poet connect the word, in a different sense, with line 13?

10 How does 'my own voice breaking' suggest an earlier time?

11 The voice the speaker hears (his own) is 'released like water' from the ear. How does this make you think of weeping, and of the physical properties of the ear?

12 The voice is 'cried from way back'. What is the poet feeling about this voice from the past? Think what 'cried' means.

13 The voice is cried 'in the spiral of the ear'. That's where it is heard – but how does the phrase connect it with the event in the past?

14 Whose voice says the last, italicised sentence? When is it said? The attitude should tell you who said it in the past. Who is saying it now?

15 Now try to make sense of how the speaker is feeling, and why. Why should the memory of his father's voice in the past, and speaking aloud the words he used, make him want to cry? Why might he find his voice 'breaking like a tear'?

Final thoughts

Now you've worked through the poem, and particularly the last stanza, read the poem again. What does the speaker feel about his father, do you think? Why do you think this?

Comparisons

You could compare this poem with:

Carol Ann Duffy
- Before You Were Mine
- We Remember Your Childhood Well

Pre-1914 Bank
- On my first Sonne
- Sonnet 130
- The Little Boy Lost/ The Little Boy Found

Homecoming

Read and revise

This is an intriguing poem to read, as much of the 'story' that produces the thoughts of the speaker is not made clear to the reader. It's the idea and feelings left after the story that the speaker, and the poet, is interested in. Read the poem once, so that the shape of the poem is in your head.

<u>1</u>   It's important to see where this poem is going, and how it's structured.

- The first stanza is not an event – it describes something. What?

- The second stanza does describe an event. When does the event take place, in the present or the past? How do you know?

- Events are described in the third stanza too, but at different times. How far apart are these times? What must have happened in the intervening years? Think about age, and the title of the poem.

- The fourth stanza is not an event, is it? There's a thought about something here. What object from the story is used in the thought?

<u>2</u>   The first line tells you that the focus of this poem is not events, but thoughts. How?

<u>3</u>   What is the first thing that you have to have in your mind, according to the speaker? What is the person who falls backwards relying on? This first thing of the two is easily forgotten about as you get involved in the events, but it's important in understanding the poem – the poet tells you so in the first line.

<u>4</u>   Lines 5–7 begin the second 'thing' to think about, the event. Where did the jacket become 'scuffed and blackened underfoot'? How does this suggest an event in childhood?

5 Look at lines 7–11, from 'Back home' to the end of the second stanza. In outlining this stage of the event, the poet uses a number of allusions (references to other things), and word plays.

- There are several 'homecomings' in the poem. Which phrase here reminds you of the title?

- The mother is described as 'the very model of a model of a mother'. How is she 'the model of a mother' – like other mothers, perhaps? 'The very model of', though, also suggests a song by Gilbert and Sullivan – 'the very model of a modern Major-General'. How might the mother be like a major-general? Gilbert and Sullivan's Major-General was also a comic figure – why might the speaker be bringing this tone into the poem? Remember this event is being looked back on.

- The mother 'puts / two and two together' means, in one way, to work things out, to make sense of something given some evidence. What does the mother want to know about?

- 'Putting two and two together' can also 'make five'. What does this phrase mean? What does 'making a fist of it' mean? Was the mother right in what she assumed, and said?

- How does 'making five' relate to 'making a fist', then 'pointing the finger'? You can see how the poet takes some common expressions, and has fun with what they mean literally.

- 'Pointing the finger' means what? Why might it result in 'Temper, temper'? Who loses their temper, do you think?

- 'Questions / in the house' refers to the child being questioned by the mother, but the phrase also makes the reader think of other 'Questions in the House'. Which house? How does this suggest the tone of the conversation, and perhaps the importance placed on the event by the mother?

- The poet isn't finished playing with words and ideas yet. What do the phrases 'seeing red' and 'Blue murder' mean? How has the poet played with what the phrases mean literally, by putting them together?

- How might 'seeing red' (by the child), and 'Blue murder', end up in 'Bed'? One inevitably ends up in the other. How does the poet use rhyme to suggest inevitability here?

6 Think about 'that exercise in trust' again, as the speaker suggested. Who has betrayed trust here? There are two ways of looking at this.

7   Lines 12 and 13 give the next stage of the event. How might being sent to bed be followed by this escape? This is where you might start to build different narratives, if you wish to. These questions might offer you different possibilities:

- Did the child simply want to run away? Why? How does 'no further than' support this interpretation of the story?

- Did the child want to ring somebody? In this case, who? Think about how the jacket might have been dirtied – or how the mother might have assumed it got dirty.

8   Lines 14 and 15 introduce 'I' for the first time, and the sixteen-year time gap. There are at least three possible interpretations of 'I', and this moment.

- 'I' is the older person – the same person, sixteen years later, coming home and having a similar, but different scene with parents.

- 'I' is the same person, sixteen years later, but now involved in a relationship with someone who he, or she, wants to ring at this moment.

- The poem is based on a relationship, and about a relationship, and 'you' have told 'I' – the speaker of the poem – about this event in childhood. Notice that 'you' and 'yours' has been mentioned three times before these lines. 'I'm waiting by the phone' is not the phone in the call-box, it's their own phone at home, waiting for the call, the start of the relationship, sixteen years after this childhood event.

Which of these interpretations do you prefer? Why?

9   Look at lines 16 and 17. Given the possible interpretations open to you, you have to think about these lines as fitting with the interpretation you prefer – or you might change your mind!

- 'Retrace' could mean simply 'go back', which the child obviously did. How might the father have wanted to 'set things straight' with the child, do you think? Is there a difference between the father and the mother?

- 'Retrace' seems to be a command here, though, meaning 'remember' or 'think about the same thing differently'. If it's 'remember', why would the father be 'in silhouette'? Remember this is sixteen years later that 'you' is being asked to remember.

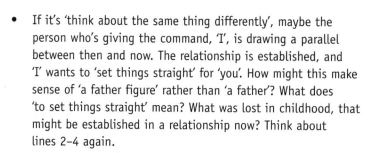

- If it's 'think about the same thing differently', maybe the person who's giving the command, 'I', is drawing a parallel between then and now. The relationship is established, and 'I' wants to 'set things straight' for 'you'. How might this make sense of 'a father figure' rather than 'a father'? What does 'to set things straight' mean? What was lost in childhood, that might be established in a relationship now? Think about lines 2–4 again.

- Whichever way you read these lines, it's about re-establishing some sort of harmony. How does the poet reflect the harmony with a rhyme? Find the word that rhymes with 'straight'.

- There's an allusion here to a famous poem, 'Maud', by Alfred, Lord Tennyson:

    'Come into the garden, Maud,
    I am here at the gate alone'.

  The poem takes place in the very early morning, and is a love poem. Another element of a romantic scene might be suggested by 'in silhouette'. What might the silhouette' be created by? Is this poem a love poem, in the end? If it is, perhaps this contributes to the overall effect.

10 Look at lines 18–21, as far as 'you say which'.

- In the last verse, 'I' is talking to 'you', apparently. Somebody is being compared to a garment – the jacket, presumably. Whose body, do you think? It could be 'you', fitting again into a childhood mould, or it could be 'I', offering to be this thing.

- Which parts of the body are clearly comparable to the parts of the jacket? The hands and fingers, though, could make different kinds of jacket fastenings. Why these parts, do you think?

- If this is 'I' making an offer, then the jacket could represent a relationship between them. What does 'you say which' suggest about the relationship – what the alternative types might be, and the attitude of 'I'?

11 'Step backwards into it' clearly reminds you of a phrase in the first verse. Which? What was that thought about? What is the speaker inviting here, therefore? The trust in childhood might have been 'blind' – is this? What is the difference?

12 'The same canary-yellow cotton jacket' makes 'you' face the object that caused the breakdown in trust in childhood, and reinvents it. The words 'there, like this' conjure up the picture of 'I' holding the

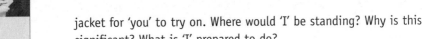

jacket for 'you' to try on. Where would 'I' be standing? Why is this significant? What is 'I' prepared to do?

13 The jacket is tried 'for size again' and 'It still fits'. In one reading, things are still the same as they were in childhood. In another, though, the jacket has come to represent trust. Trust is tried again, and fits. What sort of trust is this, though? Is it a different sort of trust, because it's a different sort of relationship? What is the speaker, 'I', offering, and reassuring 'you' about?

Final thoughts

This is a complex, allusive poem, but repays the work that is necessary to understand it. It is open to several interpretations by the reader. What do you think it is about, in the end? Even having worked through the questions above, you will still need to read it several more times to find new possibilities. Do you think it is a love poem? You might think about the title again, too – how is the end a 'homecoming'?

Comparisons

You could compare this poem with:

Carol Ann Duffy

- Before You Were Mine
- Anne Hathaway

Pre-1914 Bank

- Ulysses
- The Affliction of Margaret
- The Little Boy Lost /
  The Little Boy Found

November

Read and revise

This is a simple and personal poem about old age and death. Read it through once, thinking about the last line particularly.

1 Feelings are important in this poem. Pick out the words and phrases in the poem that tell you how John, and the speaker himself, feel about the day.

2 The purpose of this journey is made very clear. Find the line in the poem that states exactly why they have come here with John's grandma. Why has the poet written it in a very simple and factual way?

3 What does line 2 tell you about John's grandma?

4 Look at the first two lines of the second verse (lines 4–5). What does John's grandma actually do? 'Her' is used three times. What does this tell you about her?

5 Verse three (lines 7–9) describes the people they see.

- Who are the people described in lines 7 and 8, do you think?

- What is the cause of their physical state? Think about the first sentence in line 7.

- How are the speaker and John 'almost these monsters'?

6 Why do the speaker and John need to 'numb ourselves with alcohol' (line 12), do you think?

7 What do you think the 'terror of the dusk' (line 13) means? Think about what happens at dusk, which relates to what they have been thinking about time. They feel it 'begin'. What will happen?

8 'The evening, failing again' (line 14) is about the same time of day, and conjures up the same feeling. You might expect the word 'falling', though, not 'failing'. Why do you think the poet has used the word 'failing'? What is in the speaker's mind that fails?

9 'We let it happen' (line 15). Do they have a choice about letting it happen? How does this explain 'We can say nothing'?

10 The poem is divided into six verses. The first five each have three lines, but the last one only has two. How is the last verse different in its subject, too? Look at each verse, working out what it describes.

11 'One thing we have to get, John, out of this life' (line 17) has two meanings. Getting 'out of this life' usually means making a change of life, a change of direction. What does it mean here, though? What have they been thinking about life, and death?

12 Line 16 is the only line about feeling alive 'sometimes'. When do they feel alive, as opposed to feeling 'terror'? Does the poem leave you thinking about life, or death? How has the poet made you think the way you do at the end of the poem?

Final thoughts

Why has the poet chosen 'November' as the title of the poem, do you think? Of course, it might be when these events took place, but it is a suitable title anyway. Think about time in the poem, and November as a time of year.

Comparisons

You could compare this poem with:

Carol Ann Duffy
- Havisham
- We Remember Your Childhood Well

Pre-1914 Bank
- Tichborne's Elegy
- Ulysses
- The Song of the Old Mother

Kid

Read and revise

In this poem, Simon Armitage creates a persona – the voice of a fictional character. In one way, this is a poem about growing up, based on the cartoon characters Batman and Robin. In another, it's a piece of fun, which has fun with these characters and with language. Read the poem through once, enjoying the flow of the language.

1 The poet plays with clichés right through the poem. A cliché is a well-worn phrase or situation, so well-worn that it's become almost meaningless – the language and situations of cartoons and comic-books, for instance. One example is 'let the cat out on that caper / with the married woman' (lines 9–10). 'Let the cat out (of the bag)' is a language cliché – we don't think about the cat and the bag, really. 'Caper' is a word from TV crime fiction, usually light, and certainly often used in 'Batman'. The 'caper with the married woman' being taken 'downtown on expenses' is a cliché of situation. Now – read carefully through the whole poem, finding as many clichés as you can. There are a lot!

2 The quick flow and vitality of the language is part of the fun of this poem. It's created in a number of ways.

- Look at the last word of each line. What have all these words (except one) got in common – 23 of them, in fact? This partly gives the poem its 'bounce'. You can find some of the same type of words in the middle of the lines, too.

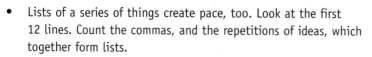

- Lists of a series of things create pace, too. Look at the first 12 lines. Count the commas, and the repetitions of ideas, which together form lists.

- Looking at the same lines, count the number of verbs. Taken together, they form a very 'active' feel.

3 What is Robin's attitude to Batman in the poem? Find evidence to support your response.

4 Look at the first three words of the poem, 'Batman, big shot'. What is Robin's attitude here? How does the alliteration of 'b' support the feeling? Say the words aloud. Alliteration is the repetition of a consonant sound to create an effect.

5 In lines 1–5, what has Batman told Robin to do? How does Batman think of this order? How does Robin think of it?

6 In lines 6–8, what does Robin now deny about his relationship with Batman?

7 Batman takes the married woman 'downtown on expenses in the motor' (line 11). Which 'motor' would it be?

8 One feature of Robin's language in the 'Batman' cartoons was the 'Holy!' exclamations – 'Holy Anthology, Batman!' Lines 12 and 13 use this form, and it's repeated to add to the listing / repeating 'bounce'. Look closely at line 12. The series of nouns sounds like a tabloid headline about a scandal. But there's more to it than that. Think about the connections from one word to the next, from 'robin' to 'egg'. How has the poet 'played' with each of these words?

9 Robin is not 'playing ball boy' any longer (line 14). How has the poet played with two different phrases here, by combining them?

10 What element of Robin's growing up is shown in lines 15–17?

11 'Now I'm taller, harder, stronger, older' (line 18).

- How do these words show Robin's feelings about his growing up? Think about the first word as well as the rest.

- What do you notice about the shape of the last four words of the line? It's an end-stopped line, too – there's a full stop at the end of the line. How has the poet made this seem like a summary of Robin's feelings?

12 Look at lines 19–22, which reveal how Robin has seen his relationship with Batman till now.

- Why will Batman be 'without a shadow' (line 20)? How has Robin seen himself, therefore? Or is this the way that he thinks Batman has thought of him?

- How does Robin perceive his role in the household till now? Does he enjoy the idea of Batman having to do domestic tasks? How do you know?

- How is 'stewing over' (line 20) a play on words? Think about what Robin means, and what Batman is doing.

13 The picture of 'punching the palm of your hand' (line 23) echoes a dramatic gesture used repeatedly in 'Batman'. Why is Batman doing it here, though?

14 Look at the last line of the poem.

- How does Robin think of Batman here? How is this change apt for a poem about growing up?

- 'I'm the real boy wonder' is apt for the end of this poem about Robin, 'The Boy Wonder'. How is he the 'real' boy wonder, though? Think about how he feels about himself now, and why.

Final thoughts

Apart from the fun of playing with the Batman and Robin characters and format, how is this a poem about young people's feelings as they grow up?

Comparisons

You could compare this poem with:

Carol Ann Duffy
- All or any poems

Pre-1914 Bank
- The Little Boy Lost / The Little Boy Found
- Ulysses
- My Last Duchess

'Those bastards in their mansions'

Glossary

* This poem is from *Book of Matches*. The title of each poem is an asterisk, meant to represent the flame of a match in a party game. Somebody has to strike a match, then tell the story of their lives before the flame burns their fingers. This poem represents the story of Prometheus.

Prometheus In Greek mythology, Prometheus was a Titan. He was known as the creator of humanity. Zeus deprived mankind of fire, but Prometheus stole it back for them. As a punishment, Zeus had Prometheus chained to a mountain. Every day an eagle tore out his liver, which grew back again by the next day.

Read and revise

This poem creates a persona – the voice of a fictional character. The poet has placed Prometheus in a modern setting, and made him the champion of mankind in a different way. Read the poem through once, thinking about the two sides here – who the speaker represents, and who is against him.

1 A sonnet is a poem with fourteen lines, with a regular rhyme scheme. The poet plays with sonnet form here – this is almost a sonnet, but not quite.

- Which lines rhyme? You should be able to find two pairs of words at the end of lines that form full rhymes.

- There are some other rhymes, though, if you look inside the lines as well. Which word rhymes with 'torches' (line 6)? Which word rhymes with 'beagles' (line 11)? Notice that they are within the verse divisions, joining things together.

- The poem is divided into four sections, unlike a traditional sonnet. Look at each part carefully, and decide what its subject is.

2 This is a poem about class. How does the poet establish the class of the speaker's opponents in the first section? How does he establish his own class? Find evidence for both.

3 What is the attitude of the speaker to his opponents in the first section? How do you know? There's more than just the second word.

4 How does the poet make the speaker's actions in the first section seem both stealthy and aggressive? Look at the verbs as well as the whole actions.

157

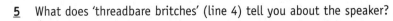

5 What does 'threadbare britches' (line 4) tell you about the speaker?

6 The 'gift of fire' (line 6) was originally given to mankind by Zeus, but then taken back again. How does the poet join the first and second sections with the idea of a gift? Who gives the gift back to the people?

7 What do 'streets and houses' (line 7) represent, do you think? How does this phrase contrast with the names for the homes of the rich in the poem?

8 What does the speaker do for the people in the streets and houses? Think about what he takes away from them, and what he seems to be encouraging them to do. Prometheus himself was eventually unchained, by Heracles.

9 How does the poet link 'cuffs and shackles' with wrists and ankles'? Think about what is being described, the sound of the words, and the shape of the lines.

10 Look at the third section (lines 10–13).

- How does the poet convey the class of the speaker's opponents in this section? Think about language as well as possessions.

- What is the attitude of the speaker to his opponents here? How do you know?

- How does the poet remind you of the Prometheus myth here?

11 The last section is the only one with a single line, and it comes after a long gap. How does the poet use the lines to create a pause before this last line?

12 Look at the last section (line 14).

- What is the last section about? How is it apt that this should be in a line on its own?

- How do the ideas of sticking to the shadows and carrying a gun fit with what has already been established about the speaker?

- The poet chooses to end the poem with the phrase 'carry a gun'. What effect does this have?

Final thoughts

The poem is based on the Prometheus myth, but this figure is not actually Prometheus. The people in the mansions behave in such a way that 'you'd think' (line 2) he was like Prometheus, stealing fire. Who do you think he might be? What sort of person? You need to have evidence for what you think.

Comparisons

You could compare this poem with:

Carol Ann Duffy
- Havisham
- Salome
- Education for Leisure

Pre-1914 Bank
- The Laboratory
- Sonnet 130
- Ulysses

'I've made out a will; I'm leaving myself'

Glossary

* This poem is from *Book of Matches*. The title of each poem is an asterisk, meant to represent the flame of a match in a party game. Somebody has to strike a match, then tell the story of their lives before the flame burns their fingers.

Read and revise

The poem is based around the idea of organ donation. The poet has fun with the idea by using some unlikely comparisons, and with rhyme and rhythm. Read the poem through once, getting the feel of the language.

1. A sonnet is a poem with fourteen lines, with a regular rhyme scheme. The poet plays with sonnet form here – this is almost a sonnet, but not quite.

   - Which lines rhyme? You should be able to find three pairs of words at the end of lines that form full rhymes, and another pair that almost does. They don't occur regularly, though.

   - There are some other rhymes, though, if you look inside the lines as well. Which word rhymes with 'brains' (line 4)? Which two words rhyme in line 12?

   - The poem is divided into three sections, unlike a traditional sonnet. Look at each part carefully, and try to decide what its subject is. You might like to come back to this when you've worked through the rest of the questions.

2. The body is full of all sorts of things. The poet has fun with the number by using lists. Look at line 3, 'the jellies and tubes and syrups and glues'. Which joining word is used three times here? Look through the rest of the poem for more lines which use the same technique – there are several. How does the poet use a variation on this in line 7?

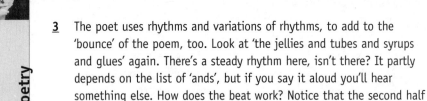

<u>3</u> The poet uses rhythms and variations of rhythms, to add to the 'bounce' of the poem, too. Look at 'the jellies and tubes and syrups and glues' again. There's a steady rhythm here, isn't there? It partly depends on the list of 'ands', but if you say it aloud you'll hear something else. How does the beat work? Notice that the second half of the line has the same rhythm as the first half. Pick out some more lines in the poem with clear, bouncy rhythms, and see how they work.

<u>4</u> The poet uses two groups of comparisons in the poem, which add to its fun, but they're appropriate, too.

- In the first section (lines 1–8) there are a series of comparisons between parts of the body and food. Pick out as many as you can. Why is the brain compared to a loaf (line 4)? Think about shape, and a common expression. Why is blood compared to 'bilberry soup'? The comparisons are all metaphors. A metaphor is a direct comparison between one thing and another, without using 'like' or 'as'.

- Why are these food metaphors oddly appropriate to describe the inside of the body?

- The last six lines of the poem use terms that usually describe clocks or watches to describe parts of the body – though no specific body parts are mentioned. The 'loops and coils' are some of these. Find as many more terms that could refer to clocks or watches as you can. There are plenty!

- How are these comparisons oddly appropriate for parts of the body, apart from the fact that they are complicated machines? Think what clocks and watches measure.

<u>5</u> Look at lines 7–8, which end the first section.

- Line 7 has three more comparisons, 'the chassis or cage or cathedral of bone'. Work out how each of these is appropriate for the body's bone structure. Think about shape, and about the other associations which each of the words has.

- In line 8, the rhythm is supported by sound repetition. Which consonant sound is repeated here? Repetition of sounds for effect is called alliteration.

<u>6</u> How does the poet signal the end of the first part of the thought of the poem, and the beginning of the second? Think about:

- the change at the beginning of line 8, marked by one word

- where the full rhyme comes here

- the punctuation before the gap
- the gap in the text
- the nature of line 9 – how is it an introduction to something new?

7   The listing reaches its peak here. How is this done? Look at the length of line, as well as joining words and alliteration.

8   The gap between the second and third sections doesn't work in quite the same way as the first gap, because it's in the middle of a sentence, with just a comma before it.

- How does the poet slow your reading down before the final thought?
- Where did the full rhyme come?
- How is the final thought marked as different at the beginning of line 13?

9   Why does the poet use the word 'ticker' to describe the heart? It's a common word to use, of course, but what does it make you think of, here?

10 'It stops or hangs' (line 14).

- How does the balance of this phrase connect with the words on the previous line?
- How does the balance of this phrase make it seem almost like a 'ticker', the word that comes before the line?
- How does this chiming poem end on a rhyme?

Final thoughts

Now you've worked through the poem, read it again, enjoying the way the poet plays with words and sounds and rhythms.

Comparisons

You could compare this poem with:

Carol Ann Duffy
- Havisham
- Salome
- Elvis's Twin Sister

Pre-1914 Bank
- Tichborne's Elegy
- Sonnet 130
- Sonnet (Clare)

Hitcher

Read and revise

This poem is a simple, if unusual, story. Read it through once, to get the whole story.

1 The tone of the poem is neutral, and factual – which is quite surprising, given the action. The poet creates the tone in a number of ways. Look at the first verse (lines 1–5).

- How many sentences are there in these five lines? Which are really short? There are no really long sentences in the poem, but when do short sentences return? Why has the poet chosen to do this, do you think?

- End-stopped lines (where there is a full stop at the end of the line) tend to stop the movement of the poem, making it seem abrupt. How many end-stopped lines are there in the first verse? Now look at the pattern of end-stopped lines in the rest of the poem. There are some throughout, but where do they become a strong feature again? Why has the poet chosen to do this, do you think?

- Look at the shape of the lines in the verse on the page. Which are the shortest lines? Which is the longest line? Is this the pattern of lines in all the verses? Think what effect this pattern has – the poem always seems to be coming to a halt.

2 You've seen that patterns in the first verse come back again at the end of the poem, when the incident is over. These are matched by a rhyme pattern, too, to reinforce the idea of things returning to normal for the speaker. Find the rhyming words in the first verse, then find the word in line 1 which rhymes with both of them. Now look carefully at the last verse, to see if you can find a similar pattern.

3 Now, look at the language of the poem.

- You might expect to find **emotive** words – words expressing emotion – in a poem about an assault. Can you find any?

- Many of the poems you have read will have a lot of imagery – pictures in words, often using comparisons, to make you feel and see what the poet wants you to. Can you find any here?

- What impression of the character of the speaker does the language of the poem create?

4 Because of the lack of emotion in the poem, the speaker's motives have to be imagined by the reader – but the poet does offer some clues.

- Look at the first three lines of the poem. What is wrong with the speaker?

- Why does the speaker attack the hitcher, do you think? Look at verse 2, and at lines 19–22. How is the hitcher different from the speaker? How is he the same? Why might the speaker find him annoying?

5 What does the speaker think about his own actions, do you think? Think about:

- line 14

- the fact that one of the things in the speaker's mind is that the hitcher 'liked the breeze / to run its fingers / through his hair'.

- the last two lines.

Final thoughts

Why do you think the poet has chosen the title 'Hitcher'? Both of the people in the poem are hitchers – look at line 4. Which one is the focus of the poem, do you think?

Comparisons

You could compare this poem with:

Carol Ann Duffy
- Stealing
- Salome
- Education for Leisure

Pre-1914 Bank
- The Man He Killed
- The Laboratory
- My Last Duchess

? Questions on Duffy and Armitage

Foundation Tier

1 Compare the ways that poets write about violence in **at least four** of the poems you have studied. Write about **The Hitcher** by Simon Armitage, **one** poem by Carol Ann Duffy and **two** poems from the Pre-1914 Poetry Bank.

Remember to compare:

- the violence in the poems
- how the poets present violence by the ways they write about it.

You might like to choose your other poems from:

Pre-1914 Poetry Bank   **Carol Ann Duffy**
The Man He Killed   Havisham
The Laboratory   Education for Leisure

2 **Education for Leisure** by Carol Ann Duffy and **Kid** by Simon Armitage offer different pictures of young people.

- Compare these two poems.
- Compare them with **two** poems from the Pre-1914 Poetry Bank.

Remember to compare:

- the young people in the poems
- how the poets present the young people in the poems, by the ways they write about them.

Higher Tier

1 Compare how poets use form, structure and language to shape meanings in **at least four** of the poems you have studied. Write about **My Last Duchess** by Robert Browning, and compare it with **one other** poem from the Pre-1914 Poetry Bank, **one** poem by Carol Ann Duffy and **one** poem from the Pre-1914 Poetry Bank.

2 In **The Laboratory** by Robert Browning and **Kid** by Simon Armitage the poets create a character through the character's own words.

- Compare the ways they achieve this.
- Compare these two poems with one poem from the Pre-1914 Poetry Bank and one poem by Carol Ann Duffy.

Remember to compare:

- the characters in the poems
- how the poets create the characters.

Pre-1914 Poetry Bank

Ben Jonson

a

> Ben Jonson (1572–1637) was one of the major writers of his age, in
> every form. He was a contemporary and friend of Shakespeare.

On my first Sonne

Read and revise

This is a simple poem about love, and grief. Read the poem once,
thinking about the effect of the boy's death on the father.

1   What was the father's 'sinne' (line 2)? How was he punished for
the sin?

2   The poem is written in rhyming couplets. The rhyming words aren't
just chosen to make a rhyme, though – they join things together.
Look at the first couplet. Why are 'joy' and 'boy' joined? Find two
other couplets in the poem where the words clearly belong together.

3   Lines 3 and 4 use the idea of lending money, and paying it back.

- How has the child been 'lent', do you think?

- What is it that has caused the payment to be 'exacted'?
  Find the exact two words that tell you.

- The 'just day' means the day when the payment is due.
  What was the 'just day' here, when the payment had to be
  made? The child is taken back. How else does the father 'pay'?
  Think about the whole poem.

4   'O, could I loose all father, now' (line 5) makes the father's
grief clear.

- The child has lost its father. How has it done this? What is the
  only way that the father could 'loose all father', then?

- The thought itself is drastic, and shows the father's despair.
  How do the words show the despair, too? Look at the last word
  of the sentence as well as the first.

5   What is the state which man 'should envie'? What state is the child
in, which the father envies? The thought is made universal, too –
it's not just the father who shouldn't 'lament' death, but 'man'. How
does this indicate the depth of the father's despair?

<u>6</u>   If man dies 'so soone' (line 7), what does he escape? What do you think 'worlds' and 'fleshes rage' might be? What 'miserie' is certain to come, if death does not come at an early age?

<u>7</u>   'Rest in peace' is often seen on gravestones. What effect does the addition of 'soft' to the phrase have (line 9)? Think about the father, and the son.

<u>8</u>   'Here doth lye' (line 9) is another phrase often seen on gravestones. Who might be 'ask'd' about the identity of the person who lies here? It's the same person who is commanded to 'Rest in peace'.

<u>9</u>   Jonson was a famous playwright and poet. How is his son 'his best piece of poetrie' (line 10), do you think?

<u>10</u> Look at the last two lines of the poem (lines 11–12).

- If the father vows to love anyone in the future, what does he hope not to do?

- Why doesn't he want to 'like too much' from now on? Think about how he feels about his son, and what the death of his son has done to him.

Final thoughts

How has the death of his son affected the father? Think about his whole state of mind as it is revealed in the poem.

Comparisons

You could compare this poem with:

Heaney and Clarke	Duffy and Armitage
• Mid-Term Break	• Before You Were Mine
• October	• 'My father thought it ...'
• Cold Knap Lake	• 'Mother, any distance greater than a single span'

W. B. Yeats

a — W. B. Yeats (1865–1939) was one of Ireland's leading poets.

The Song of the Old Mother

Read and revise

This is a simple poem about the daily chores of the 'old mother'. Read it through once, noticing how she feels about young people.

<u>1</u> The first four lines of the poem are about the old mother's daily life.

- Her life is hard. List the physical activities she mentions here.
- Is the old mother the first person in the house to rise? How do you know?
- How long is the old mother's working day? How do you know?

<u>2</u> Lines 4–8 describe 'the young', from the old mother's point of view.

- How does line 5 show a contrast with the old mother's life?
- What sorts of things do the young think about, compared to the old mother's concerns?
- Line 7 tells you that their days are not as busy as the old mother's. Which word in the line reminds you that this reflects the old mother's attitude? What is her attitude to the young?
- What does line 8 say about the young? How does the way that the thought is expressed reflect the attitude of the old mother to the young?

<u>3</u> Line 9 summarises the old mother's attitude to her life. What exactly is it? Think about each word in the line, and about what has gone before: the attitude to the young, and the repetition here of the word 'must'.

<u>4</u> The form of the poem echoes the nature of the old mother's life – it helps to shape the meaning.

- How does the rhyme scheme work? Is it regular, like the old mother's life?
- Is the rhythm of the lines regular, or irregular? Try saying any line aloud – can you hear a clear beat?
- Look at lines 1 and 3, where the mother lists her actions and tasks. Which word is repeated several times? How does this use of form mirror her life and work?
- Look at line 2. Where is the form of this line repeated almost exactly later in the poem? It makes the poem seem almost circular. How does this use of form mirror the old mother's life and work?

<u>5</u> Look at the last line of the poem.

- How does this line suggest the end of the day? Look back at the first and second lines.

- The choice of this as the last line suggests more than just the fire going out. Who in the poem might get 'feeble' – and in that case, what would 'cold' imply?

- How does the rhyme here support the idea of the fire going out suggesting more than just the end of the day? Think which words are connected by rhyme.

- The flames of the fire are described as 'seed' in the poem, twice. Why has the poet chosen this comparison, do you think? What does it compare the fire to, and how might you connect this with the old mother's life?

Final thoughts

Read the poem again. How do you feel about the old mother, at the end? What has made you respond in the way you do?

Comparisons

You could compare this poem with:

Heaney and Clarke	Duffy and Armitage
• Digging	• We Remember Your Childhood Well
• Catrin	• 'My father thought it ...'
• Baby-sitting	• 'Mother, any distance greater than a single span'

William Wordsworth

a

William Wordsworth (1770–1850) was one of England's greatest poets. He was made Poet Laureate in 1843.

The Affliction of Margaret

g

Glossary

undone	ruined
beguiled	deceived
ingenuous	simple, natural
apprehensions	anxieties, fears

Read and revise

This is a poem about a woman in despair, because she does not know where her son is. Read the poem through once, taking in as many of her anxieties as you can on first reading.

1 'My apprehensions come in crowds' (line 64). There is no particular order to the thoughts and fears that Margaret expresses in the poem. Each verse deals with an aspect, or aspects, of her worries, but they are presented in an almost random order. Why has the poet chosen to do this, do you think? How does it mirror Margaret's state of mind?

2 Look at the first verse (lines 1–7).

   • Look at the phrase that is repeated in lines 1 and 2. Why has the poet chosen to repeat this? What does the repetition show about Margaret's state of mind?

   • Throughout the poem, Margaret imagines where her son might be, and what has happened to him. Three possibilities are mentioned in lines 3 and 4. What are they?

   • What does Margaret wish for, if her son is dead? When would she be at rest, and not thinking of her son with either blame or sorrow?

3 The second verse tells you how long Margaret's son has been gone, and about some of her feelings.

   • What different feelings has she felt during this time that are mentioned in this verse?

   • What might she have 'believed'?

   • What thoughts does she 'catch at', and miss?

   • What 'darkness' is Margaret referring to, do you think?

4 In the third verse, how did Margaret feel about her son before he left? How does she feel about the way she brought him up? Are there any hints that her son was not as perfect as she says?

5 In the first verse, Margaret mentions feelings of 'blame' and 'sorrow'. In the fourth verse (lines 22–28), is she blaming the Young One (all Young Ones, really) for causing distress? Is the focus of her thoughts on the Young One, or on the Mother?

6 In the fifth verse (lines 29–35), what 'wrong' has Margaret imagined that her son has done to her? What effect did the thought have on her? What is she proud of about her own behaviour?

7 Look at the sixth verse (lines 36–42).

   • Why does Margaret imagine that her son might not want to come home? What does she protest that she doesn't value?

- Lines 41 and 42 are intriguing. Why should the son think of her 'with grief and pain' (line 39)? She says that she 'now can see with better eyes' (line 40). Better than when? What has she said to her son in the past, do you think?

8 In verse seven (lines 43–49), Margaret thinks about how far away her son might be.

- How are birds, 'the fowls of Heaven', who also fly away, lucky?

- The birds go up to the sky – but what might happen on 'land and sea'?

- All that might be left behind are 'wishes'. Are the wishes likely to be fulfilled, according to Margaret? What does this tell you about her state of mind?

9 The eighth verse (lines 50–56) offers three of Margaret's fears about her son.

- What are the three fears?

- How might the first fear mentioned here have followed from verse seven?

- How do the words the poet chooses in lines 50 and 51 convey Margaret's emotions?

- In line 55, why does the poet repeat the word 'Thou'? What does it tell you about Margaret?

- Why is the sleep of the dead sailors described as 'incommunicable'? Think what Margaret longs for.

10 How does the thought of the dead communicating (or rather, not communicating) lead to the ninth verse? Why does Margaret 'look for Ghosts' (line 57)? If there were communication of this sort, who would Margaret 'have sight of'? There are two possible interpretations here.

11 The tenth verse (lines 64–70) outlines the effect of the son's absence on Margaret's mind. What does she fear? What is she certain of? How has her despair affected her view of the world?

12 The last verse touches the depths of Margaret's despair.

- She feels that she is alone, and can't be helped. Why can't she? Look carefully at lines 71–74.

- What friend does she feel that she has? How is this a measure of the hopelessness of her situation?

Final thoughts

The poem is called 'The Affliction of Margaret'. What is Margaret afflicted by, exactly?

The poet has revealed the feelings and the character of Margaret through her own words. What do you feel about and think about Margaret in the end? How has the poet made you respond in the way you do?

You could compare this poem with:

Heaney and Clarke
- Mid-Term Break
- Catrin

Duffy and Armitage
- Havisham
- 'My father thought it ...'
- 'Mother, any distance greater than a single span'
- We Remember Your Childhood Well

Comparisons

William Blake

a

William Blake (1757–1827), poet and artist, published *Songs of Innocence*, from which these poems are taken, in 1789. It was his second publication, and its underlying theme is the presence of divine love and sympathy, even in trouble and sorrow.

The Little Boy Lost / The Little Boy Found

g

Glossary
mire   mud
nigh   close by

Read and revise

These two poems should be read as one. They are simple, and almost child-like, with some mysterious touches. Read the poems once, to take in the simple story.

1   Why do you think the poet begins the first poem with the little boy's voice? How does it make you respond to the boy, and to the father?

2   The form of the poems is fairly simple, which suits the story.

- How many beats are there in the first and second lines in each verse, and in the third and fourth? Work them out by saying them aloud, or hearing them in your head. How does this seem like something being made simple?

- Look at the fourth verse. Which lines rhyme? Look back at the third and second. Which lines rhyme? How does this achieve a sense of completion each time?

- The first verse is different, though. You know which words should rhyme. Do they? If this is only an echo, why doesn't the poet choose to have a full rhyme here? What sort of feeling is being expressed?

3   In the second verse, what are the problems that the little boy has? What is the effect on him?

4   The 'vapour' in line 8 of **The Little Boy Lost** and the 'wand'ring light' in line 2 of **The Little Boy Found** is a light or spirit of some kind, as shown in Blake's illustrations for the poems. How does the little boy respond to the light? Why, do you think?

5   In line 3 of **The Little Boy Found**, how is God aware of the boy's plight? What does this tell you about the poet's ideas?

6   In line 4, why should God appear 'like his father'? Why does he appear 'in white'? What associations does this colour have?

7   Look at the final verse of **The Little Boy Found**.

- How does God's behaviour differ from the boy's father's?

- How do the boy's parents' behaviour and emotions differ?

- In line 7, why is the mother 'pale', do you think?

- Why is the dale described as 'lonely'? Who is lonely, actually? How does describing the dale as 'lonely' add to the effect?

- There's a rhyme in line 7. Which two words rhyme? How does this add to the emotional effect of the line?

Final thoughts

One interpretation of these poems, supported by Blake's illustrations, is that the 'Father' in the first poem is a priest, educating the boy in organised religion, and leaving the boy behind. He is rescued by God, and by his mother, who is Mother Earth. Read the poems again carefully, considering this interpretation. Can you find evidence from the poems to support it?

Comparisons

You could compare this poem with:

Heaney and Clarke	Duffy and Armitage
• Follower	• We Remember Your Childhood Well
• Baby-sitting	• 'My father thought it ...'
• Cold Knap Lake	• 'Mother, any distance greater than a single span'

C. Tichborne

a

C. Tichborne wrote this poem the night before he was executed for his involvement in a plot to assassinate Elizabeth I in 1586. He was only 28 years old.

Tichborne's Elegy

g

Glossary

tares	weeds
a shade	a ghost; unreal
My glass is full; and now my glass is run	refers to the sand running through an hourglass

Read and revise

1 Look at stanza one.

- The poem begins with Tichborne's central feeling that he is in his 'prime of youth'. What ought he to be feeling about his life, instead of the 'frost of cares' that he feels it has been? What does frost do?

- Look at line 2. Underline the two words in the line that are opposites. The line works through a metaphor – a direct comparison. What does he compare his 'joy' with?

- Now look at line 3. Underline the word that suggests good things, or richness, and the word that suggests the opposite, then look at the whole comparison in the line.

2   The poet makes us feel his despair by saying the same thing over and over, in different ways. The form of the poem helps the reader feel this by using a lot of repetitions.

- How are lines 1–3 similar? Which words are repeated?

- Work out the rhyme scheme in stanza one – which last words rhyme? Now look down the other two stanzas – the rhyme scheme is repeated. Which line is identical in each stanza? What effect does the repetition have?

3   Each fifth line in the poem is a **paradox**. In stanza one, how is the poet's 'day' past? What is his life being compared with?

4   Look at stanza two. Pick out all the contrasts.

- Which line do you think is at the heart of the poet's feelings?

- In what way has the poet not been 'seen' yet?

- Look at line 11. How is his 'thread' about to be cut? In what way isn't his thread completely 'spun' or finished yet?

5   Now look at stanza three. It has a growing sense of despair, and things coming to an end.

- The poet has already suggested that his life is ending prematurely. According to line 13, when did his death begin?

- Look at line 17. Think about his first 'glass' as referring to a wine glass – what is that saying about his life? Think about the second 'glass' as referring to an hourglass. If his glass is 'run' (out), what is that saying about his life?

6   How does the poet deliberately reinforce the sense of repetition in this last stanza? Look at line 16, and think how it prepares for the last line of the poem.

Final thoughts

There isn't much progression of thought in this poem – it's almost like one statement, repeated over and over. Why has the poet done this? Read it through again, noticing all the repetitions of thought and form.

<table>
<tr><td rowspan="4">**Comparisons**</td><td colspan="2">**You could compare this poem with:**</td></tr>
<tr><td>**Heaney and Clarke**</td><td>**Duffy and Armitage**</td></tr>
<tr><td>• Mid-Term Break</td><td>• Havisham</td></tr>
<tr><td>• October
• Cold Knap Lake</td><td>• November
• 'I've made out a will; I'm leaving myself'</td></tr>
</table>

Thomas Hardy

a Thomas Hardy (1840–1928) was one of the great novelists of the late nineteenth century, and also a distinguished poet.

The Man He Killed

g

Glossary

nipperkin	a small measure of beer
'list	enlist (in the army)
traps	personal belongings
quaint	odd, strange

Read and revise

This is a simple poem in its thought and language, but there is a difficulty for the speaker. Read the poem through once, noticing where the hesitation comes.

1 This poem creates the voice of a character, as if the person was speaking to you. This is indicated by the speech marks in the poem, but by other means as well.

- Which words in the poem have been chosen because they belong to spoken language? Find several examples.

- We tend to hesitate or repeat ourselves more in spoken than in written language. Can you find examples of hesitations or repetitions in the poem? How has the poet used punctuation to indicate them to the reader?

2 The form of the poem seems fairly simple, which matches the simple voice and thought.

- Work out the rhyme scheme – which lines in each verse rhyme?

- The rhythm of each line in the verses is the same – more or less. Work it out, and read right through the poem. Are there any lines where it seems slightly different? Which? You might already be identifying the area where the poem changes a little.

3 How does the first verse simply state the 'curious' thing about the man he killed? What is 'curious', exactly?

<u>4</u> The second verse (lines 5–8) states what has happened to the two men.

- How does line 7 make the two men seem the same? Think about the balance of the line as well as what it means.

- He killed him 'in his place' (line 8). What does this mean on the battlefield, do you think? What other 'place' does the speaker think about twice in the poem, where things would have been different?

<u>5</u> Look carefully at the third verse. Up to this point, the speaker has simply given facts, but now some uncertainty appears.

- Why is there a hesitation after 'because' in line 9, do you think? What does it show? How has the poet created it? Think about punctuation and the line.

- How does the repetition of 'because' in line 10 add to the feeling of the speaker's difficulty?

- In line 11, the speaker reassures himself three times that he shot the man because he was 'my foe'. Find all three instances.

- Line 12 begins with another reassurance. Why do you think the man has had to reassure himself four times about his reason for killing the man?

- Why is this the only verse that doesn't end with a full stop? Think about uncertainty. What effect does the gap created after 'although' have? Think about the stress on the word, and the pause it creates when you read it.

<u>6</u> The fourth verse (lines 13–16) shows how similar the two men were.

- How were the two men the same?

- Which phrase in line 14 makes really clear the man's difficulty in seeing 'the man he killed' as his foe?

- There was 'no other reason' for the men enlisting than those given in the verse. What other reason might there have been for enlisting? Why does the absence of any other reason make the killing more difficult for the man to justify?

<u>7</u> In the last verse, line 17 sums up the man's feelings about war. What do the last two lines of the poem show about the nature of this man, who has just killed somebody?

Final thoughts

If there is a message in this poem, what do you think it is? Don't be tempted to make a snap judgement – think about it.

You could compare this poem with:

Heaney and Clarke
- Mid-Term Break
- The Field-Mouse

Duffy and Armitage
- Salome
- Education for Leisure
- Hitcher
- 'Those bastards in their mansions'

Walt Whitman

a

Walt Whitman (1819–92) was an American poet, born in New York.

Patrolling Barnegat

g

Glossary

Barnegat Bay	a bay on the New Jersey coast
demoniac	demonic, devilish
combs	the breaking tops of waves
trinity	a group of three

Read and revise

This is a lively poem, full of sound and movement (like the sea). Read it through once, enjoying the sound and movement.

1 The poem is about the people who patrol the beach in the storm, but they are not identified until nearly the end.

- Which phrase in line 13 finally identifies people?

- Although the people are not identified until line 13, they are described before this. Line 8 describes them as 'watchful'. Work through the rest of the poem from this word to the end, finding all the words that describe them. What picture emerges of these people? How does the poet feel about them, do you think?

2 This is a poem in free verse – there is no set pattern of rhythm. There's a lot of rhythm within lines, though, and one repeated feature of language that creates rhythm. What is it? Look at the ends of the lines. How does this feature make the poem seem full of action, too?

3 The first four lines of the poem have the same pattern: a noun and an adjective at the beginning of the line, then the verb at the end.

- In line 1, why do you think the word 'wild' is repeated? Think about the effect of this at the beginning of the poem.

- What do you notice about the three words at the end of line 2, 'incessant undertone muttering'? Count the syllables in each word, and remember that onomatopoeia is the term to use when describing words that match the sound of the thing they're describing.

- What are the 'Shouts of demoniac laughter', do you think?

- Another technique is used to convey the sounds of the water and waves in line 3. What do you notice about 'piercing and pealing'? Remember that alliteration is the word to use to describe the repetition of consonant sounds to create a particular effect.

- What is the 'savagest trinity' in line 4?

4 The next two lines, 5 and 6, describe places.

- Identify the alliteration in line 5.

- Look at line 6. There's an obvious alliteration here – look at the number of times 's' starts a word. Look at the first six vowel sounds in the line, though – they're all different. Why do you think the poet has chosen to do this? Think about the nature of the storm, and the sounds it produces. Look back at the first two words of the poem, too.

5 Lines 7 and 8 introduce the watchers.

- It is the watchers who are 'breasting' the wind. Which words in line 7 make their task seem difficult, and dangerous? What do these words suggest the poet feels about them?

- Identify the alliteration in line 8.

6 Line 9 is different from the rest of the poem – it's in brackets, and gives voices and questions.

- Whose are the voices, do you think?

- Why do the voices have to ask questions? What does this suggest about the conditions in the storm?

7 Lines 10–12 describe the progress of the patrol.

- Line 10 is about **touch** – the 'slush and sand of the beach' as the patrol walks. Line 11 features **sound**, the 'hoarse roar', and line 12 is all about **sight** – what the watchers see. Look back through the poem, noticing where the poet appeals to touch, and sound, and sight.

- Identify the alliteration that appears at the beginning of each of lines 10 and 11, and the one in line 12.

- The last four words are a repetition of the last four words in line 5. Why has the poet chosen to do this, do you think? Think about 'never remitting' in line 11.

8 Look at the last two lines of the poem.

- Why are the forms 'dim' (another use of **sight**), do you think? What does it suggest about the conditions?

- How has the poet emphasised the difficulty of their task in line 13? Notice the form of the two verbs in the line. How is this repetition of verb form appropriate for the end of the poem?

- Why has the poet chosen 'watching' as the last word of the poem, do you think?

Final thoughts

You've picked out a lot of alliteration in the poem. Which letter has featured most often? Why do you think the poet chose to repeat this one? Remember what the poem is describing.

The poet uses a lot of techniques in this poem. Read it again, taking in the cumulative effect of them all – the way they make you see and hear the violent activity of the storm.

Comparisons

You could compare this poem with:
Heaney and Clarke
- Storm on the Island
- Blackberry-Picking
- Death of a Naturalist
- October
- Cold Knap Lake

William Shakespeare

William Shakespeare (1564–1616) was a leading Elizabethan playwright, but also a great poet as demonstrated in the sonnets that he wrote. This is number 130 of 154 sonnets.

Sonnet 130

Glossary

dun	slightly brownish dark grey colour
damasked	damask is a firm, lustrous fabric or it can mean a two-toned colouring
reeks	is breathed out
belied	shown to be false

Read and revise

This poem is about love, and writing – how comparisons used by lovers are often unrealistic. Read it once, noticing the change of tone at the end of the poem.

1 Look at the first line of the poem.

- Most of the poem is based on denying romantic comparisons. What is the first comparison Shakespeare says is untrue?

- Which two words make this denial strong? Say the line aloud, and notice where the stresses fall.

2 The first line deals with eyes, and the second, lips. Look quickly through the rest of the poem, identifying the features described.

3 What does the second line deny about the lips?

4 The sonnet is written in iambic pentameter – lines of five beats, where the stress falls on every second syllable in the line. The second line isn't quite regular, but you can see that stresses fall on 'far', 'red', 'her', and 'red'. Why has the poet chosen to emphasis 'far' in this way? Why is 'her' emphasised?

5 What does line 3 deny about the breasts? How does the poet create a balance in the line, using the stresses? Think about the colours.

6 Line 4 is slightly different. The poet agrees that his mistress's hair is like wire. If he were trying to be romantic, what might he compare her hair to?

7 The first four lines of the poem each deal with a different feature of the poet's mistress, but the next eight lines are organised in four pairs, each pair describing a feature. Which feature are lines 5 and 6 about? Which romantic comparison is denied?

8 What romantic idea is denied in lines 7 and 8? Which word in line 8 is deliberately strong, to attack the idea of 'perfumes'?

9 Although the poem seems anti-romantic in the first eight lines, in the end it's a love poem too. How does this become apparent in line 9? Which word does the first stress in line 9 fall on? What romantic comparison do lines 9 and 10 deny, nevertheless?

10 Which romantic comparison do lines 11 and 12 deny? Although she isn't a goddess, what does 'treading on the ground' say about his mistress? Is it as bad as her breath 'reeking'?

11 The poem changes at line 13.

- How is the thought in lines 13 and 14 different from the rest of the poem? Work out exactly what the lines mean. Why does the poem end on the idea of 'false compare'?

- How does the poet indicate the strength of his feeling for his mistress in line 13? On which words do the stresses fall? Why are these words important to hear at this moment in the poem?

- The last two lines are inset. This was a conventional device for a sonnet – but how is it appropriate here?

- Look at the rhyme scheme of the poem. How are the last two lines different from the rest? How is the change, and the rhyme, appropriate for the ending?

Final thoughts

Do you think this is an effective love poem, or not? Why?

Comparisons

You could compare this poem with:
Duffy and Armitage
- Anne Hathaway
- Before You Were Mine
- 'Mother, any distance greater than a single span'
- 'My father thought it ...'
- 'I've made out a will; I'm leaving myself'
- 'Those bastards in their mansions'

Robert Browning

Robert Browning (1812–89) was a prolific poet. He wrote a number of dramatic monologues in verse, including this poem.

My Last Duchess

g

Glossary	
Ferrara	The poem is based on the life of Alfonso, Duke of Ferrara in the 16th century, whose wife died after three years of marriage. The specific incident is imagined, however.
all one	all the same
munificence	generosity

Read and revise

This poem creates a persona – the voice of a Duke, whose character is revealed through his own words.

The poem imagines the Duke showing a portrait of his 'last Duchess' to a visitor, the emissary of a Count. Read the poem through once, just concentrating on the story about the Duchess that the Duke tells, and forming your first impressions of the Duke himself.

1 The Duke speaks to 'you'. It's not apparent until line 49, though, that 'you' means the Count's emissary. When you first read the poem, who does 'you' seem to be? What effect does this have on the way you engage with the poem?

2 The first line of the poem immediately conjures up the situation – you can imagine the Duke pointing to the picture. The line sounds like speech, too – 'That's ...' Look through the poem and find at least three more phrases that are clearly chosen to make the words sound like somebody speaking.

3 'Looking as if she were alive' (line 2) has two meanings, once you've read the whole poem. What are the two meanings?

4 The Duke calls the 'piece' a 'wonder' (line 3). It's his 'piece', or possession, of course, and has the name of a painter (evidently famous) attached to it. How does the Duke want the emissary to think of him, having such a thing? What other possessions and names does he mention in the poem? Think about this carefully.

5   Is line 5 an invitation or an instruction, do you think? Remember the social status of the two people.

6   The Duke comments that he mentioned Frà Pandolf 'by design' (line 6). What does this reveal about him?

7   Part of the design of the poem is that the reader comes to a view of the Duchess as well as the Duke, through what he says about her – and partly in spite of his views. What does line 8 make you think about her?

8   How do lines 9 and 10 emphasise the Duke's importance, in his own eyes? As well as the meaning of the words, think about which words in the lines are stressed by the natural 'beat ' of the lines.

9   How does 'if they durst' (line 11) reflect the Duke's view of himself?

10   How does the poet make the sentence that begins in line 13 sound like an announcement? What, according to the Duke, should have been the only cause of joy for the Duchess?

11   What does the description of the Duchess in lines 17–19 make you think about her? Which word in line 19 shows the Duke's contempt of compliments to his wife? How does the poet stress the word by its placement in the line?

12   How did the Duchess react to the compliments? Look at lines 20 and 21. How does the Duke continue to show his contempt in these lines?

13   Look at lines 21–24, from 'She had ...' to 'went everywhere.' What did the Duke dislike about her? Reading between the lines (you have to do this a lot with this poem, if you don't trust what the Duke says), what do these words say about the Duchess, do you think?

14   In lines 25–31, the Duke complains that the Duchess was too free with her approval, and did not differentiate between things.

- What does 'My favour at her breast' reveal about the Duke's attitude to his relationship with his wife?
- What does line 27 tell you about the Duchess's effect on other people?
- 'The approving speech, / or blush, at least'. What does this tell you about the Duchess?

15   What do lines 33 and 34 reveal about the Duke's sense of his own importance?

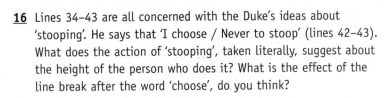

16 Lines 34–43 are all concerned with the Duke's ideas about 'stooping'. He says that 'I choose / Never to stoop' (lines 42–43). What does the action of 'stooping', taken literally, suggest about the height of the person who does it? What is the effect of the line break after the word 'choose', do you think?

17 The Duke says that he has no 'skill / In speech' (line 36). Has he?

18 Lines 37–39 reveal what the Duke would have liked to say to his wife, if it hadn't meant 'stooping' to do it. What do the words in speech marks reveal about the Duke's attitude?

19 'If she let / Herself be lessoned so' (lines 39–40). What does 'lessoned' imply about the Duke's attitude to his wife, in his eyes? 'Lessoned' sounds like another word, though, especially when spoken aloud, as this appears to be. How would the Duchess have been 'lessened', or diminished, actually?

20 Look carefully at lines 45–47.

- What did the Duke 'give commands' to do? What does this reveal about him?

- 'Then all smiles stopped together', taken one way, reveals the effect on the Duchess's behaviour? What was it, do you think? Taken another way, though, it means something much more sinister. What?

- 'There she stands / As if alive' comes as a shock, especially as it is placed immediately after the sentence about smiles stopping. What possibilities are raised now? How has the poet increased the effect on the reader of 'As if alive', by placing it where he does?

21 There's a full stop after 'alive' (line 47), but no line break – the duke apparently continues to talk without a break. What does this reveal about him? Remember what he's going on to talk about.

22 The Duke says that the Count's daughter is his 'object' (line 53), or aim. What indications are there in lines 49–51, though, that something else is more important to him? Find particular words as evidence. How does the poet make the remark about 'his fair daughter's self' in line 52 seem like an afterthought?

23 Look at the last sentence of the poem, from 'Notice Neptune' (line 54) to the end.

- Why do you think the poet chose this particular statue for the Duke to value? Think about 'Taming a sea-horse'.

- How does the Duke emphasise the statue's value – and therefore his own wealth and importance?
- Why do you think the poet choose to end the poem on the words 'for me'?

Final thoughts

Now that you've looked at the detail of what the Duke says, reflect on the first line of the poem again. What does the line reveal about the Duke now?

What do you think of the Duke, and the Duchess, now that you've worked through the poem? Think about how the poet has led you to respond in the way you do, when you only hear the Duke's words.

You might have thought that the Duke was jealous. What was he jealous of, exactly?

Comparisons

You could compare this poem with:
Duffy and Armitage
- Havisham
- Salome
- Education for Leisure
- Kid
- 'Those bastards in their mansions'

The Laboratory

Glossary	
ancien régime	The poem's setting is in the 'ancien régime' – pre-revolutionary France – and imagines an incident in the life of Marie Madeleine Marguerite D'Aubray Brinvilliers (1630–76). She poisoned her father and two brothers and planned to poison her husband.
pastile	a small cone of aromatic paste, burnt to scent or fumigate a room
minion	a dainty person
morose	gloomy or sad

Robert Browning The Laboratory

185

Read and revise

This second poem by Robert Browning creates a persona – the voice of a woman, whose story and character are revealed through her own words. Read through the poem once, working out what the woman wants to do, and why, and forming your first impression of her.

1 The poem takes the form of the spoken voice – the woman is speaking to the chemist who is mixing the poison for her. Looking at the first verse, how does the poet suggest the presence of the chemist, and how does he make the words seem like speech? Think about:

   • what the chemist is doing
   • how he is addressed
   • the question asked.

2 Now look through the rest of the poem, looking for more evidence of the same things.

   • Work out what the chemist does during the 'action' of the poem.
   • Look for more questions addressed to the chemist.
   • Look for exclamations that seem to be addressed to the chemist.

3 In the first three lines of the poem, how does the poet quickly set the scene? What do you already know, by the end of line 3, of the people, place, things and atmosphere?

4 How does line 4 come as a surprise, even though it is so early in the poem? How does the poet underline the directness of the question, and the woman's intention?

5 The reader has to piece together what is going on from the woman's words, and never knows all of it. Who are the 'he' and 'her' of line 5, do you think? Does it matter that you're never completely sure about their relationship with the speaker?

6 The woman is clearly obsessed with the relationship between the two other people, and in verse II the obsession in her mind is shown by the way she repeats things – obsession means that you go over things again and again. Beginning from 'they know that I know' (line 5), how many repetitions can you find in verse II? Think about words, phrases and the shape of phrases.

7 What does the woman think that the other two people think about her? Where does she think that they think that she is? How does the poet make 'I am here' emphatic? Where is she, and why does she say it so emphatically, do you think?

8 Look at the first two lines of verse III.

- Which are the words that identify what the chemist is doing? Do you think the woman is describing what he is doing, or commanding him?

- Work out which words the stresses in this line fall on, by saying them aloud. What do you notice? What effect does the stressing have on the feeling in the woman's voice?

9 Look at lines 15 and 16. What are the adjectives and adverb in these lines? How do they contrast with the word 'poison'? What does this tell you about the woman's mind?

10 In verse V, what does the word 'pleasures' reveal about the woman's nature? How does the poet convey her excitement? Think about sentence forms, lists, and punctuation.

11 Look at verse VI.

- What does the woman imagine herself doing in this verse?

- 'He' and 'her' are identified in verse II as the objects of the poisoning – but who are 'Pauline' and 'Elise'? Even if one of them is 'her', the other one isn't. Who is the woman she is thinking of, do you think? What does it reveal of her nature?

- The woman lists Elise's 'head / And her breast and her arms and her hands'. Why does she do this, do you think? What does it reveal about her?

12 In verse VII, what does the exclamation 'Quick' tell us? What does line 27 tell us? What is she looking forward to enjoying?

13 Look at verse VIII.

- How does the woman indicate that there is not enough poison yet? Find two phrases as evidence.

- How does she insult the other woman – twice?

- What does 'say, 'no!' / To that pulse's magnificent come-and-go' mean? Think what a pulse does.

14 Look at verse IX.

- What does she imagine that her gaze might have done to the other woman the night before?

- How has the poet drawn your attention to the word 'Shrivelled'? Think about the gap that's created before the word, and the pause after.

15 Look at verse X.

- What does 'let death be felt' mean? What does it tell you about the woman?

- What does she want to happen to the other woman's face? Why?

- What is the alliteration in line 39? Alliteration is the repetition of a consonant sound to create an effect. What is the effect? What does it tell the reader about the woman's feelings?

16 In verse XI, why does the woman want to have her mask removed, even though it might be dangerous? Why does she think the poison can't hurt her?

17 What does line 45 reveal about the woman, do you think? Why has the poet identified the chemist as an 'old man'?

18 At the end of the poem, the woman is looking forward to dancing 'at the King's', whereas at the end of line 12 she was reluctant to go. How does the poet show her eagerness? What has changed? What does her desire to 'dance' at this moment reveal about her?

Final thoughts

Now you've worked closely through the poem, what is your response to the woman's character and behaviour? Think about all the methods the poet has used to create this character through her own words.

Comparisons

You could compare this poem with:

Duffy and Armitage

- Havisham
- Salome
- Education for Leisure
- Kid
- 'Those bastards in their mansions'

Alfred, Lord Tennyson

Alfred, Lord Tennyson (1809–92) was one of the great poets of the Victorian era. He was Poet Laureate from 1850 until his death.

Ulysses

Glossary

Ulysses The Latin name for Odysseus, the Greek hero whose travels from Troy to his home on the island of Ithaca is the subject of Homer's Odyssey

an aged wife Ulysses' wife, Penelope

mete and dole give out in small quantities

unequal not equal to the task; perhaps unjust

lees the sediment in wine. To 'drink to the lees' means to the last drop

Telemachus Ulysses' son and heir

rainy Hyades a group of stars which rise with the sun in spring at the rainy season

the Happy Isles the islands of the blessed, thought to lie beyond the Pillars of Hercules (Gibraltar)

Achilles Greek hero, who killed the Trojan hero Hector

Read and revise

In this poem Tennyson creates a persona – the voice of the great Greek hero. In the poem Ulysses is an old man who has returned from the wars and at last been restored to his rightful position. Read the poem through once, to get the feel of Ulysses' state of mind.

1 Now that Ulysses is at rest, he is unhappy.

- In the first five lines, what things are mentioned that make him discontented? How do these things contrast with the life he has led?

- What is the significance of the word 'still' (line 2)? What does it reveal about Ulysses?

- The islanders 'hoard, and sleep, and feed, and know not me' (line 5). What is wrong with them, in Ulysses' view? How has the poet created Ulysses' tone of contempt? Listen to where the stresses fall in the line.

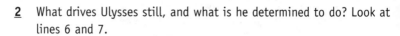

2 What drives Ulysses still, and what is he determined to do? Look at lines 6 and 7.

3 'All times I have enjoyed / Greatly, have suffered greatly' (lines 7–8). How does Ulysses' past life contrast with his life on the island, when you think about this statement? How does the poet emphasise the extremes of Ulysses' past? Think about where words are positioned in the line, as well as the repetition.

4 What do you think Ulysses means when he says 'I am become a name' (line 11)?

5 Ulysses says he has a 'hungry heart' (line 12). What is he hungry for?

6 Look at the sentence beginning 'Much have I seen' (lines 13–17). What has Ulysses enjoyed? Include what he says about himself in line 15. Why do you think the plains are described as 'ringing'?

7 What do you think Ulysses means by 'I am a part of all that I have met' (line 18)? How is this true of everybody?

8 Lines 19–21 express a difficult idea, but one that is central to understanding the character that the poet has created.

- Picture the arch in your mind – after all, that's how a metaphor works, by comparing one thing with another in a picture. The arch is made of what has already happened. Beyond the arch, there's a horizon. How does the horizon 'fade' when you move towards it?

- How do you know that the idea of the arch, and moving through it (which is what an arch is for) is attractive to Ulysses? Think about 'Yet', and two of the words in line 20.

- Look at the beginnings of each of these lines, too. Why has the poet placed these words at the beginnings of lines?

9 What does Ulysses find 'dull' (line 22)? What does Ulysses compare himself to in line 23, and what does this reveal about how Ulysses sees himself?

10 'As though to breathe were life' (line 24). What is life for Ulysses? Why isn't 'to breathe' enough? Think about his life on the island again.

11 Look at lines 24–28, from 'Life piled on life' to 'A bringer of new things'. What is the 'eternal silence' Ulysses is aware of? What does he want?

<u>12</u> Look at lines 28–32, from 'and vile it were' to 'of human thought'.

- How long does Ulysses think he has left?

- Why do you think the idea of having 'to store and hoard' himself is 'vile' to Ulysses?

- What does Ulysses want?

- Why is knowledge 'like a sinking star'? Think about the arch again, and perhaps about Ulysses' life too. A simile is a comparison between two things, using 'as' or 'like', as here.

<u>13</u> Look at the third section of the poem, from lines 33–43, which describes Ulysses' feelings about his son.

- Ulysses praises his son. Pick out all the words in the section that are words of praise.

- The tone of this section is quite different to the rest of the poem, as though Ulysses is not quite saying what he means. Which words here could not apply to Ulysses himself? How is Telemachus different from Ulysses?

- Which sentence sums up the difference between the two men?

<u>14</u> The tone of the final section (lines 44–70) is different again. What is the tone of this section, do you think? Think about:

- Ulysses' state of mind here

- the effect of 'My mariners' (line 45) and 'Come, my friends' (line 56)

- the effect of the last six lines.

<u>15</u> What is in Ulysses' mind in lines 44 and 45?

<u>16</u> This poem is in **blank verse** – the lines are largely iambic pentameters, but they do not rhyme. The poet has chosen words that rhyme in line 46, however – 'wrought' and 'thought'. Why do you think he has made this choice here? Remember that rhyme connects things.

<u>17</u> Look at lines 49–53, from 'you and I are old' to 'strove with Gods'. How does this repeat an idea from earlier in the poem? Find the lines where the idea occurred earlier.

<u>18</u> Look at lines 54 to 56.

- Identify the sounds and sights in these lines.

- Line 54 seems like an invitation, perhaps. How? What is the dominant vowel sound in this line?

- Look at the vowel sounds in the sentence beginning 'The long day'. There are two assonances here – repetitions of vowel sounds to create effect. What are they? Look at all the sounds, though – are they long vowels, or short? What is the effect of them, taken together? Does the tone of the poem deepen, or lighten? How is the effect apt for this moment in the poem, do you think?

19 What idea is Ulysses still hanging on to in line 57?

20 How does line 58 show Ulysses back in action, and in command again? Think about the positioning of the key words in the line.

21 Why are the furrows 'sounding', do you think? You might need to research what an ancient Greek sailing ship was like – it wasn't like the drawing in the Anthology.

22 Where is Ulysses going to sail to? Think about the arch again.

23 'Wash us down' (line 62) refers to Homer's idea of the ocean as a river encompassing the earth, and on the west plunging down a vast chasm where the entrance of Hades was. In lines 62–64, what is Ulysses anticipating?

24 Look at the last six lines of the poem, from 'Though much is taken' to the end.

- The tone of these lines depends partly on a mixture of balance and strength. In lines 65–67, what things are balanced? How is the balance reflected in balanced phrases? Which?

- Which phrases in lines 66 and 68 reflect their great deeds in the past?

- What two things are balanced in line 69?

- The rhythm of the lines in the poem varies considerably, but in the last two lines it is regular and strong. Say it aloud, or hear it in your head as you read it. Notice which words the stresses fall on. Why these words? What ideas are being stressed? Why has the poet chosen to make the rhythm so clear and strong at the end of the poem, do you think?

- The last three words are 'not to yield'. What does this tell you about Ulysses? What is he determined not to yield to?

Final thoughts

Now you've worked closely through the poem, what is your response to Ulysses' character? Think about all the methods the poet has used to create this character through his own words.

This poem was written in 1833, soon after the death of Tennyson's close friend Arthur Hallam. Tennyson wrote that the poem showed his 'resolution to overcome the mood of despair' and that it 'gave my feeling about the need of going forward, and braving the struggle of life'. How does the poem show these things, do you think?

Comparisons

You could compare this poem with:

Heaney and Clarke	Duffy and Armitage
• Follower	• Havisham
• Mali	• Education for Leisure
	• Homecoming
	• November
	• Kid

Oliver Goldsmith

a

Oliver Goldsmith (1730–74) was a writer of prose, poetry and drama, and became most famous as a playwright. This poem is taken from 'The Deserted Village', published in 1770.

The Village Schoolmaster

g

Glossary

furze	a wild shrub, also called gorse
counterfeited	false
aught	anything
cipher	work out by arithmetic
presage	forecast
owned	admitted to

Read and revise

1 How do the first two lines remind you that this poem is part of a larger poem that describes a whole village?

2 The furze is described as 'unprofitably' gay. What does this suggest about the amount of blossom, and how does it help to form the picture? The larger poem is partly about the arrival of new wealth from trade into agricultural communities, and the consequent departure of the peasants. How might this word refer to this idea, in some way?

3 Which word in line 3 is the first that actually describes the master himself? How does this word set the tone of the whole description?

4 In line 5 the master is described as 'severe' and 'stern'. Find examples from the whole poem of the master being 'severe' or 'stern'.

5 Which word is used four times in lines 6–11? What does this repetition emphasise about the relationship between the master and his pupils? Why might this reflect particularly a village school?

6 Look at lines 6–12.

  • Like 'skilled to rule' (line 3), which phrase in line 6 sets up an idea, which is then shown in a number of ways?

  • 'Boding' in line 7 probably means the 'tremblers' are worried about what might happen, as in 'foreboding'. Why are they 'boding tremblers', though? What might 'the day's disasters' (line 8) be, do you think?

  • What does 'counterfeited glee' (line 9) mean, do you think, and why do the 'boding tremblers' laugh in this way?

  • Does the phrase 'for many a joke had he' suggest that the master was a funny man, or not? How do the 'boding tremblers' know when to laugh, do you think?

7 'Yet he was kind' (line 13) looks like the beginning to a new aspect of the master. What examples of this can you find? What does this suggest to you?

8 How does the speaker excuse the master's severity, in line 14? Which word in this line is the key idea for the following four lines?

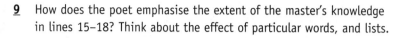

9 How does the poet emphasise the extent of the master's knowledge in lines 15–18? Think about the effect of particular words, and lists.

10 Lines 19 and 20 appear to praise the master's skill in argument. Are there any implications here that might make you think that the master is not being praised unconditionally?

11 Look at lines 21 and 22. Is it the master's skill in arguing which impresses the 'gazing rustics', or something else? What does this imply about the master?

12 Look at the last two lines of the poem.

- How does line 23 appear to be working up to a heroic conclusion? Think about the way the poet has used repetition, and the way the line is balanced.

- In one way, the last line is a simple statement of admiration. Is there any way to read this line differently, though? Think about who is making this assessment, and how they are described, as well as the line itself.

Final thoughts

Now that you've worked through the poem, look back at how the poet has introduced several ideas, and run them through the poem. There's only one full stop in this poem, at the end. Why has the poet chosen to do this, do you think?

The poem is a description of the village schoolmaster. How do you respond to him, in the end? How do you think the speaker, and the poet, want you to respond? Are there different ways of viewing the man, based on the evidence in the poem?

Comparisons

You could compare this poem with:

Heaney and Clarke
- Follower
- Digging
- Catrin

Duffy and Armitage
- Before You Were Mine
- Kid

Alfred, Lord Tennyson

a Alfred, Lord Tennyson (1809–92) was one of the great poets of the Victorian era. He was Poet Laureate from 1850 until his death.

The Eagle

g **Glossary**

azure sky blue

Read and revise

This is a short and apparently simple poem, but the poet has used considerable skill to describe the eagle. Read the poem though at least twice, listening to the rhythm and hearing each word.

1 The poem is divided into two verses of three lines. How are the two verses different in content? What different aspects of the eagle do they describe?

2 The three lines of each verse end with a full rhyme – a **rhyming triplet**. Why has the poet chosen to do this, do you think? Is the eagle in harmony with his surroundings? How?

3 The rhythm also creates a sense of harmony.

   • How many beats are there in each line? You can hear the rhythm very clearly in line 1.

   • The beat falls on the second, fourth, sixth and eighth syllable in lines 1, 4, 5, and 6. It isn't quite the same in lines 2 and 3, though. How are the beginnings of these lines different?
   Say them aloud, or hear them in your head as you read. Which words stand out, because the rhythm is different? Why does the poet want to emphasise these words in his description of the eagle, do you think?

4 Look at the first line of the poem. Which sound is repeated three times in this line, then again in line 2? Why has the poet chosen words so that this sound can be repeated, do you think? Think about the nature of the sound, and the nature of what the poet is describing. Remember that the repetition of consonant sounds to create an effect is called alliteration.

5 What are the eagle's 'crookèd hands' (line 1)? How does this direct comparison with hands help you to picture the eagle?

6 How is the eagle 'Close to the sun' (line 2)? How is it 'in lonely lands'?

7 From which angle would the eagle appear to be 'Close to the sun' and 'Ring'd with the azure world'? Think of the point of view, or the camera angle if the eagle were being filmed.

8 How does line 3 make the eagle seem powerful and important? Think about the point of view again, and the effect of 'Ring'd' – what is in the centre of the ring?

9 How does the point of view, change in line 4? This makes sense of the verse change, too.

10 Why is the sea described as 'wrinkled'? Think about angle. What does the word suggest about the height the eagle is looking from? How does 'crawls', as a description of the sea's movement, add to this impression?

11 How does 'from his mountain walls' (line 5) imply the power and security of the bird? Think about 'his' and 'walls' particularly.

12 'Like a thunderbolt' (line 6) obviously describes the speed of the bird's flight. How does it also suggest the bird's power? What sort of power is it?

Final thoughts

It's surprising how much skill is packed into this short poem. Read it again, noticing how each word and phrase adds to the picture.

Comparisons

You could compare this poem with:
Heaney and Clarke
- Perch
- Death of a Naturalist
- A Difficult Birth . . .
- The Field-Mouse

Gerard Manley Hopkins

a

> Gerard Manley Hopkins (1844–89) was a poet of considerable originality, particularly in the use of rhythm.

Inversnaid

g

Glossary

burn	small stream (Scotland), often coloured dark brown from peat
coop	a hollow place, enclosed
comb	the top of the water
fell	fiercely
degged	sprinkled
groins	structures that prevent water eroding land
braes	hillsides (Scotland); 'groins of the braes' are probably paths by the burn
flitches	ragged brown tufts (of bracken)
ash	the mountain ash, or rowan, has clusters of red berries
bereft	deprived, robbed

Read and revise

The poet uses language in a very concentrated, intense way in this poem. Read through the poem once, noticing particularly the sounds of the words.

1. Look at the first verse. What sights and sounds does the poet make you see and hear? Sights include colours, of course.

2. Look at the first two lines of the poem.

   - The poet partly uses one and two syllable words to create rhythm. Thinking about this, work out the rhythm of these two lines. How many beats are there in each line? How are the lines balanced, both with each other and in themselves?

   - The poem is full of alliterations – repetitions of consonant sounds to create effect. What alliterations can you find in these two lines? Is the letter in line 2 heard twice, or more?

   - Why do you think the burn is described as 'horseback' brown? Think of the associations of a horse that might fit the nature of the burn, as well as the colour.

- 'Rollrock' is an invented word. How does it capture the movement and nature of the burn?

3   Look at lines 3 and 4.

- There are three alliterative words in these two lines. Find them. Which alliteration appears in both lines? Now look through the next two verses for more examples of this alliterative sound. You should find several. Why has the poem chosen to use this letter so often? Think about the sound of the burn.

- The rhythm of these two lines is the same as the first two – count the beats – but also different. How many two syllable words are there in these lines?

- In the first three lines the first stress comes in the second syllable – on 'coop' in line 3, for example. In the fourth line it's different, though. Which word does the first stress fall on? Why do you think the poet wants to bring this word out?

- The foam on top of the water is compared to a 'fleece'. Why do you think the poet uses this word? How is the foam like a fleece? Think of at least two reasons.

- What does the word 'flutes' suggest about the sound the burn makes?

4   Lines 5 and 6 describe the froth on the top of a pool.

- Why is the froth described as a 'windpuff bonnet', do you think? Think about each element of the phrase.

- 'Turns and twindles' is another alliteration – but what do you think 'twindles', a word which the poet has invented, might mean? Think about the words that might have been combined to make this new word.

5   Lines 7 and 8 describe how black the pool is. The idea of line 8 is that the pool is so black that even Despair (a black mood) would drown in it. There are two alliterative words in the line again. Find them. The vowel sounds are more significant here, though. Which vowel sound occurs three times in the line? What does the repetition of the sound convey about the movement of the water in the pool? Repetition of vowel sounds for effect is called assonance.

6   Look at the third verse (lines 9–12), which describes the land on the side of the burn.

- How does the poet create balance in line 9? Think about the rhythm, and the repetitions. The 'wildness' (line 15) is in harmony with the 'wet' of the burn.

- Line 10 looks like the longest line of the poem on the page – and if you count the syllables, you'll see that it is. There are still the same number of stresses in the line, though. Say it aloud or hear it in your head, and count them. How does this line make the movement of the burn seem like a 'tread'?

- Why does the poet create the word 'beadbonny' for the ash, do you think? What are being compared to beads? How does the ash 'sit over' the burn?

7 Think about the structure of the poem now. How are the first three verses different from the fourth verse? Think about the different sort of writing in the fourth verse from the first three.

8 Look at the last verse (lines 13–16).

- Look at the phrase 'Of wet and of wildness' in line 14. How does the poet play with the words in the following two lines?

- Look at line 13. How does the poet use alliteration in this line to set up the sound that is going to run through this verse?

- What is the poet's plea about the 'wildness and wet'? How does he emphasise the depth of his feeling about this sort of place?

- Typically, the poet pulls together the thought of the last verse using alliteration. What alliteration is there in the line? How do the words reflect the preceding three lines of the verse?

Final thoughts

The poem is complex, in the sense that the poet has combined closely a number of techniques in a relatively short poem. The message in the end is simple, though. Read the poem again, thinking how the intense description of the first three verses leads to the thought in the fourth verse.

Comparisons

You could compare this poem with:
Heaney and Clarke
- Storm on the Island
- Perch
- Blackberry-Picking
- Death of a Naturalist
- At a Potato Digging
- A Difficult Birth . . .
- The Field-Mouse

John Clare

John Clare (1793–1864) was the son of a Northamptonshire labourer. He was largely a poet of rural life.

Sonnet

Glossary

Mare blobs	another name for the water buttercup or marsh marigold – a plant with tiny yellow flowers that grows in ponds
flag	reed grass

Read and revise

This is a simple poem – it has a simple thought at its heart, and expresses it clearly and in a straightforward manner. The poem works only on sight – what the poet sees. Read through the poem once, seeing in your mind the things he sees.

1. This poem is a sonnet – a poem of fourteen lines with a regular rhyme scheme. As befits the whole poem, the rhyme scheme is very simple. What is it?

2. The first four words set the tone and content for the poem. Which two words set the tone? Which two words set the content?

3. 'I love' is a simple expression of how the poet feels about this time of year. Look down the first words in each line of the poem. How many times does the poet use this formula, including one variation? How does this maintain the simple form?

4. The poem has no punctuation at all. How does this add to the sense of natural simplicity?

5. What season is the poem set in, exactly? Look at the first and third verses, and find evidence of exactly what stage of summer the poet is describing.

6. In line 2, the poet compares the clouds to 'white wool sacks'.

   - How is this an appropriate description for the clouds?

   - The comparison with wool keeps the poem rooted in nature, too – how is this appropriate for the poem?

   - How is the same thing present in line 1? Think about the word 'beaming'. What is the summer being compared to?

<u>7</u> Which colours does the poet use in lines 4 and 5? The verbs 'stain' and 'whiten' are both active verbs – there is a process being described. What is the process that is happening? Think back to your response to Question 5.

<u>8</u> The reed clumps rustle 'like a wind shook wood' (line 6). How is this comparison typical of the poem? Look back to Question 6.

<u>9</u> In line 7, how does the poet emphasise an action again? Look where the verb is placed.

<u>10</u> Which word in line 8 reinforces the time of year that this poem pictures? How?

<u>11</u> Look at the description of the willow in lines 9 and 10.

- How does the poet make the picture really exact, so that you can picture the tree exactly?

- Although the poem works through sight, the poet uses sounds of words to create pictures too. Which vowel sound is repeated at the beginning of line 10? Find the same sound in line 9. How does this sound relate to the lake? The repetition of vowel sounds to create an effect is called assonance.

<u>12</u> Now look at the last two lines, which pull together some of the ideas in the poem.

- The word 'bright' is repeated in these lines. How does this remind you of the opening of the poem?

- The 'clear lake' is also a repetition. How does it relate to the idea of brightness and light?

- 'Play' as the last word of the poem, and 'sport' (meaning play) in the previous line introduce a new idea at the end of the poem. How does it contribute to the feeling of the poem about this time of year?

Final thoughts

Read the poem again, enjoying its simplicity. Do you prefer simple poems like this, or more complex poems such as **Inversnaid**?

Comparisons

You could compare this poem with:

Heaney Clarke

- Storm on the Island
- Perch
- Blackberry-Picking
- Death of a Naturalist
- A Difficult Birth . . .
- The Field-Mouse

Comparing poems / Structuring a poetry response

As you can see in the sample questions, and in 'How the English Literature *Anthology* fits into the course' (page 71), you will be offered three questions to choose from for each pair of poets. Each question will name at least **one** poem, and you will have to compare **one** poem by each of your chosen poets and **two** poems from the Pre-1914 Poetry Bank.

You might be asked to compare meanings in poems, such as the feelings and attitudes in them, or the poets' ideas, and you'll be asked to compare the style of the poems – the way the writers have used form, language and structure to express meanings. That sounds a bit forbidding, but if you've worked through some of the poems, you'll already have a good idea of what this means.

Of course, there are a lot of questions that could be asked on each pair of poets, and any number of combinations of poems you could choose to tackle the questions. Below is an example of the sort of choices you might make in response to a specific question, and how you might plan a response – in rather more detail than you might do in an examination, but it will indicate the sort of things you might compare. The plan is in a table. Suppose the question you had chosen to attempt was:

Compare the ways that poets write about nature in **four or more** of the poems you have studied. You should write about **The Field-Mouse** by Gillian Clarke and **Storm on the Island** by Seamus Heaney, and **two** poems from the Pre-1914 Poetry Bank.

Remember to compare:

- what the poets write about
- the methods they use to write about nature.

Two poems from the Pre-1914 Poetry Bank that would be good choices here would be **The Eagle** and **Sonnet**. The bullets here simply remind you about the Assessment Objectives. You could write about each poem in turn, comparing as you go, but you are far more likely to hit the top criteria in comparison if you can hold the four together. The sections offer you a perfect way to do it, looking for similarities and differences in content first, then in style. Here are some notes for a possible response.

The Field-Mouse	Storm on the Island	Sonnet	The Eagle
What the poets write about: Aggression connected with nature			
People aggressive towards nature, causing 'hurt', 'agony', bleeding', and to each other, 'gunfire'	'pummels', 'hits', 'bombarded'	**Sonnet** is different and shows not aggression but passive enjoyment – 'beaming', 'sailing', 'happy', 'bright'	'like a thunderbolt he falls' both **The Eagle** and **Storm on the Island** show unstoppable power in nature
Feelings caused by nature			
The Field-Mouse has feelings of responsibility for damage – 'the killed flowers', 'ought to finish it off'	Fear of nature in **Storm on the Island** – 'the thing you fear'	love of nature in **Sonnet** – 'I love to see'	Admiration for eagle – 'like a thunderbolt'
Other issues			
The Field-Mouse has political thought, unlike others			**The Eagle** not personal, unlike others
The methods they use to write about nature: Language			
Imagery of war / combat in **The Field-Mouse**: look closely at lines 1 –2, 25–27	Imagery of war / combat in **Storm on the Island**: look closely at lines 16–18	Positive language in **Sonnet**. Natural imagery, not military, in **Sonnet** 'white wool sack'	**The Eagle** only poem not first person

continued

The Field-Mouse uses hayfield deaths as metaphor for war – others not as ambitious as this	Negative language in **Storm on the Island**. Heaney for hardness	Alliteration used by Tennyson ('clasps crag', etc.). Clare uses alliteration / assonance for brightness. Simple diction of **Sonnet** v rest of poems	
Structure			
The Field-Mouse progresses through day to dream at night	**Storm of the Island** a progression – carefully stepped to reflect growing fear	Pre-1914 poems simpler. **Sonnet** simply a list	Pre-1914 poems simpler. **The Eagle** angle below / angle above
Form			
The Field-Mouse uses blank verse. **The Field-Mouse** in three stanzas	**Storm on the Island** uses blank verse. **Storm on the Island** in one long stanza	Pre-1914 poems simpler. Clare sonnet form, rhyming couplets	Pre-1914 poems simpler. **The Eagle** two 3-line triplets

Prose

The *Anthology* Short Stories

If you are studying the *Anthology* Short Stories rather than a novel for Section A of the English Literature examination, the following pages will guide you through each of the stories. It's important to remember that the same Assessment Objectives are tested for the short stories as for the poetry – so, as well as knowing what you think about the stories and understanding how the writers have worked in the writing of the stories, you will need to be ready to compare the stories too.

Doris Lessing

a Doris Lessing was born in 1919. She lived in Africa from 1924 until 1949, when she moved to England, with the manuscript of her first novel, which became a best-seller. She has won a number of literary prizes, including the WH Smith Award in 1986.

Flight

g **Glossary**

frangipani   a tropical tree with white scented flowers
sardonic   gloomily scornful or mocking

Read and revise

Read the story right through once, focusing on the old man's emotions.

1   The author (and perhaps the old man) clearly connect the granddaughter with the favourite pigeon. Look at paragraph one and find the words that describe this bird. Think how they might apply to the girl as well.

2   Find the one word in paragraph two that sums up the old man's mood. Now look at paragraph five, beginning 'His mood shifted.'

   • Find the words in this paragraph which identify his mood now, and notice the change from paragraph two.

   • What has caused the change in mood?

   • With your knowledge of the whole story, what does the action of shutting the bird into its box represent? Look at what the old man does, and what he says. Look up **symbol** in the Glossary (page 251).

3   Read the short paragraph beginning 'Hey!' (line 25). Which words tell you about the girl's attitude to her grandfather at this point?

4   Look at the brief conversation between them, beginning 'Waiting for Steven' (line 28). Look for the attitudes and feelings here. What does the phrase 'curling like claws' remind you of?

5   Look at the two sentences beginning 'Misery went to his head' (lines 38–40). Find the single words about the old man and the girl which contrast directly with each other.

6 Look at the paragraph that begins 'Growling' (line 45). What reasons can you see here for the old man feeling and behaving in the way he does? Which words tell you this?

7 Read the conversation between the old man and his daughter (lines 72–100). What is his daughter's attitude to him? Look at what she says to him, the way she's described, and how she speaks. Which of the two seems the older here?

8 The grandfather says to his daughter, 'Can't we keep her a bit longer?' What does this tell you about the relationship between them? Who has the greater authority in the household?

9 Look at the paragraph beginning 'Do you like it?' (line 107)

- How are the girl and Steven behaving towards the old man? Find the words that describe their feelings, their attitude, their intentions.

- Why are their eyes described as 'lying', do you think? What have they suggested that might not be true?

- Who do you think is describing their eyes as 'lying'? The grandfather? The author? Or the young people themselves?

- Is the girl's affection a lie? Think about the last sentence of the story.

10 The girl advises her grandfather that he should 'shut up' the new bird 'until it knows this is its home'. Why is it ironic that she should say this? Look at your responses to questions 2 and 5. Think again about the girl's reaction at the end of the story.

11 Look at the phrase 'Released by his half-deliberate anger' (line 118). Steven and the girl now feel free to move away from him.

- Why has the author chosen the word 'released' here, and why has she placed it at the beginning of the sentence and the paragraph?

12 In the paragraph beginning 'Released', how does the old man see the young couple now? How does their behaviour make him feel?

13 'They had forgotten him again. Well, so they should' (line 122). In terms of the development of the old man's emotions, how is this an important moment?

14 The paragraph ends 'and took out his favourite'. The author does not say 'his favourite pigeon'. Why not? What is she indicating here?

15 ' "*Now* you can go," he said aloud. He held it poised, ready for flight, while he looked down the garden towards the boy and the girl. Then, clenched in the pain of loss . . .'

- Why '*Now*'? Think about your response to question 13.
- The old man clearly knows what releasing the bird will represent. Think about where he looks before he releases it, and think why releasing a homing pigeon (which he knows will return) causes him to feel 'the pain of loss'.

16 '... the whole afternoon had stilled to watch his gesture of self-command' (lines 133–4). What has the old man made himself do?

17 Find the single word in the next short paragraph that conveys his mood as he looks up to the sky. How is this a change from earlier in the story? Why has his mood changed, do you think?

18 Look at the description of the birds flying, from 'The cloud of shining silver birds' to 'the shelter of night' (lines 137–143).

- Find all the words here which refer to or suggest light and shade and make a distinction between them.
- Which type of word (light or shade) has the author used to refer to the sky, and which to the ground?
- Which type of word has the author used to refer to release, and which to coming home?

19 Look at the description of the girl in the last paragraph.

- Referring to your response to the previous question, how does the author continue the light / shade idea here, and what does she suggest through it?
- Why do you think the girl is in tears as she looks at her grandfather? What do you think she may have realised as she watched the birds?

Final thoughts

Read the story right through again, this time looking at the girl's emotions and how they change. Compare the development of her feelings to the changes in her grandfather's emotions. Why has the situation reversed?

Consider how you feel about the grandfather at the end of the story, and how you felt about him at the beginning. How has Doris Lessing made you change your view, and your expectations?

? Questions

Foundation Tier

Flight and **Your Shoes** both show an older person wanting to restrict a younger member of the family. Consider both stories. You should write about:

- the older people's reasons for wanting to restrict the younger people
- how the young people respond to their situations
- how the authors show the feelings of both the older and younger people
- who you sympathise with, and why.

Higher Tier

In **Flight** Doris Lessing uses pigeons as a symbol of something else. Write about how she does this, and how the writer of another story from the Anthology uses the same technique. You should write about:

- the symbols and what they represent
- why the writers have chosen these particular symbols
- how the writers show that these things are symbols
- what the writers gain from using the symbols.

Sylvia Plath

a Sylvia Plath was born in 1932 in the USA. She married the English poet, Ted Hughes, in 1956 and settled in England. They separated in 1962; a year later she committed suicide. She wrote this autobiographical story while she was still at college.

Superman and Paula Brown's New Snowsuit

g

Glossary

Dali   Salvador Dali was a surrealist painter, whose most famous pictures showed collections of objects associated with dream-like symbols in bold, colourful landscapes.

Icarus   In Greek legend Icarus was the son of Daedalus, an Athenian craftsman. To help them to escape from prison in Crete, Daedalus made wings so that he and his son could fly over the sea. But Icarus flew too close to the sun and, when the wax on his wings melted, he fell into the sea and drowned.

Read and revise

This story is quite complex. Read it right through once before tackling any of the questions.

1   Paragraph one mentions 'the changing colours of those days'.

- Look at paragraphs two and three, and find all the words that mention or suggest colours or light. Notice how many there are.

- Now look at the last paragraph of the story. Find all the words that mention or suggest colour. Which period of the narrator's life do the bright colours belong to?

2   Look at paragraphs two, three and four, down to 'the motors of a thousand planes'.

- Find all the words that suggest excitement, myths and fairy tales.

- Now find all the words that refer to dreams and flying.

- You should now have found a lot of words in the first four paragraphs. If you look at them together, what do they tell you about the narrator's feelings about her childhood?

3   In paragraph three, the narrator remembers 'making up dreams'. What is she able to do with these dreams?

4 Look at lines 41–6. What unpleasant things are mentioned here?

5 Now look at the short paragraph beginning 'The threat of war was seeping in everywhere.' (lines 65–68)

- Find references to both play and war here.

- Why do you think Sheldon 'became a Nazi'? (Look back at question 4.)

6 Look at the paragraph beginning 'The movie was about ...' (lines 88–91). In the second sentence, how does the writer emphasise that this was something very different from the imaginary world of childhood? Look at the shape of the sentence as well as the words that are used.

7 In the film the Japanese soldiers are shown torturing the prisoners, and killing them and laughing. Who else in the story have we already seen behaving like this?

8 When the narrator goes to bed after seeing the war film, and closes her eyes, she sees very different pictures in her mind from those she sees at the beginning of the story. How are they different? What can't she do now?

9 The second part of the story begins with 'Saturday was bitterly cold ...' (line 103). It's about a children's game. Look at the first sentence beginning 'Saturday' and underline all the adjectives. What sort of mood is being created here?

10 Find the moment when Paula falls over, and look at the two sentences beginning 'No one said a word.'

- There's a reminder of the beginning of the story here. What is it?

- How does the author create a sense of something coming to an end in the second sentence? Find all the words that help to suggest this. (Think about what a window blind does.)

11 When the other children look at the narrator, they have 'a strange joy' (line 129) in their eyes.

- What does this remind you of, earlier in the story?

- What do you think the author is suggesting here about the nature of children?

- Do you think this can be extended to human nature in general?

12 Now read right down to 'Only tell me how it really happened' (line 173). Do you think Mother and Uncle Frank believe the girl? What details make you think they do, or don't?

13 Read the next paragraph where the narrator says she 'can't make it any different'. Why can't she? How is this different to what she used to be able to do?

14 Read to the end of the story. You've already noticed how the dominant colours in the last paragraph are different from the colours at the beginning.

- Can you now say why they are different? What do the dark colours represent?
- How are you reminded of the early paragraphs here?
- 'Nothing held, nothing was left.' Of what?
- '... and the real world, and the difference'. What do you think these words mean, and why does the author end with them?

Final thoughts

Read the whole story once more, thinking about the title. How do the two things, 'Superman' and 'Paula Brown's New Snowsuit', symbolise the 'difference' in the narrator's life that came about during this period?

Questions

Foundation Tier

How do **Superman and Paula Brown's New Snowsuit** and **Flight** show some of the difficulties of growing up? You should write about:

- the difficulties the central characters have with other people
- how they feel about the difficulties they face
- how the writers of the stories show their difficulties
- differences between the stories.

Higher Tier

Several of the stories in the Anthology are about moments in people's lives when they realise something important. Compare **Superman and Paula Brown's New Snowsuit** and one other story of your choice, showing how the authors of the stories reveal these moments. You should write about:

- the realisations that the people in the story come to
- the experiences they have which lead to the realisations
- how the writers use language and structure to present their experiences
- differences between the stories.

Michèle Roberts

a ── Michèle Roberts is half-English and half-French. She was poetry editor of the feminist magazine *Spare Rib* from 1975 to 1977.

Your Shoes

Read and revise

There's a lot to look for in this story. It's written as a first-person narrative that begins as a letter from a mother to her runaway daughter – though you may wonder if it's still a letter by the end. Read the story right through before looking at any of the questions.

1 The woman reveals a lot about herself and her past.

- Look first at the paragraph beginning 'Your father didn't mean it' (line 53). Which words are used here to describe the woman's family, and her father?

- Look through the rest of the story for instances of what she had to do when she was a child, and what she couldn't do.

2 The woman's relationship with her mother was clearly very difficult, and affected her considerably.

- Look for some of the criticisms she has of her mother, and notice how the writer suggests them.

- 'There was so much I wanted to say to her and now it's too late' (lines 94–95). Why didn't she say these things to her? What is she doing now, in effect?

3 The woman's relationship with her father might seem easier than that with her mother. Find some examples of her preference for her father. But it's not as simple as that. Read from the paragraph beginning 'I had a white wedding' (lines 134–152).

- What would her father have done to her if he'd known the truth about her?

- What didn't he do for her when she was a baby, and why?

4 Her own marriage is not quite what it seems.

- What feelings did she not experience at her wedding? Find the sentences that describe it. Look for the sentence in paragraph five (lines 28–30) that describes how a 'husband and wife' should behave. What does this reveal about the woman's relationship with her husband?

- Now look at the paragraph beginning 'I don't think you have a clue how we feel' (line 76). What don't this couple do? Think about the way the woman describes her own childhood and what the connection might be.

- 'After all this is his house' (lines 92–93). What does this comment reveal about the woman?

5   The mother has a number of conflicting emotions about her child. Look for examples of:

- her criticism of her daughter's behaviour
- her lack of understanding of her daughter
- her jealousy of her daughter.

6   Look at the paragraph beginning 'Of course I wanted you' (line 142).

- How does the mother see herself here?

- What did she not do for her child? (Think about what she's doing now.)

- How did she try to be a good mother? Find some examples.

7   Look at the last nine lines of the story (lines 183–191). What emotion does the woman feel most strongly now? What does she want to do for her daughter? Do you think she's ever revealed this before?

8   The writer shows us the woman through a first person narrative, so that we follow her thoughts and feelings.

- Sometimes feelings are stated directly, such as 'I might go mad'. Find another example of a direct statement of emotion in the story.

- In other instances the reader has to decide whether the first person narrator is reliable – do you believe her? In the paragraph beginning 'Your father didn't mean it' (line 53), she writes, 'We've given you everything a child could possibly want'. Is this true? Do you think she believes it?

9   The woman in the story is in a state of extreme grief. 'If I wrap my arms around myself and hold tight it keeps the pain in ... If I keep my mouth pursed tight I can't scream or throw up' (lines 19–21).

- What does she want to do with her pain? Think about her life when she was younger and living at home, then her married life.

- What does she do during the story, actually?

10 The writer uses shoes in all sorts of ways in the story, including in the title. Look up the definition of symbol in the Glossary (page 256).

- At the end of the story the woman behaves in a very unusual way with the shoes, but the reader has been prepared for this. 'Someone ... might pick up a shoe from the rug and hold it like a baby' (lines 6–7). 'I locked the door on those rebellious shoes' (line 11). Who is being identified with the shoes here?

- 'They're best in here with me, I think, safe and warm in bed. Tucked up tight' (lines 165–66). Who are the shoes representing (or symbolising), and at what age?

11 Perhaps the shoes don't just represent one person. What is it that the woman, her mother and her daughter all have in common? Think about the exact physical position the woman ends up in. She's curled up, enclosed, and sucks the laces of the new shoes. What does this resemble? What are the shoes a symbol of now?

Final thoughts

This is a complicated, sophisticated story. Take a break from it, then read it again, thinking about these two issues:

- 'It didn't do me any harm' (line 58). What harm was done to the woman in her childhood?

- There are a number of possible interpretations of the ending. Is it a positive ending, or a negative one? Is the woman sliding into madness, or coming to terms with something? It might help to look closely at what she says, thinks and feels here – in ways that perhaps she has never done before.

Questions

Foundation Tier

The mother in **Your Shoes** and the grandfather in **Flight** both
become very distressed about certain events that take place.
Compare how the distress of the characters is shown. You should
write about:

- the causes of their distress
- how they deal with it
- their situations
- how the authors use language and structure to explain
  their situations
- differences between the stories.

Higher Tier

Several of the stories in this section deal with strong emotions.
Compare **Your Shoes** and **one** other story from the Anthology which
does so. You should write about:

- the emotions that are shown in the stories you have chosen
- how the authors convey these emotions to the reader.

Joyce Cary

a Joyce Cary was an English writer who lived from 1888 to 1957. Several of his novels deal with the gradual change in the social and political structure of modern England.

Growing Up

g

Glossary

primeval	from the earliest ages
langour	dreamy relaxation, laziness
languid	lacking energy or enthusiasm
Paleface	the native American term for a white man
iodine	a type of disinfectant

Read and revise

Read the whole story through once, focusing on the way Robert's feelings about his daughters change.

1 Robert is unhappy about a number of things in his life. The first of these things is suggested in the first paragraph. What is it, and how do you know?

2 Throughout the story things do not happen as Robert expects. What is the first indication of this, in the second paragraph?

3 The next five paragraphs, up to 'Hullo, hullo, children' (line 25), are all about the garden, which suggests that it is important in the story in some way. The garden is described as 'a wilderness'. Look through the five paragraphs, and pick out the things that are 'wild' in the garden.

- The parents hoped that the children 'should do what they liked' in the garden. How does this relate to the rest of the story?

- Quick prefers the 'wild' garden to the 'shaved' and 'combed' gardens of his neighbours? Think about the end of the story, and what Quick seems to prefer by then.

- Read again from 'It had come to seem, for him ...' (line 17) to the end of line 25. What words and ideas in these lines suggest that Robert's view of the nature of the garden is imaginary rather than realistic? What might this have to do with the view he has of his children, and how that view changes in the story?

- Robert sees the garden as 'free' nature. Which two words in the last of these paragraphs connect with this word? What do you think Robert wants to be 'free' from?

- Robert likes the idea that the garden has the suggestion of 'primeval' forests. What 'primeval' instincts are released in the garden later, and how does Robert respond to them?

4   The next six paragraphs, from 'There was no answer' (line 26) to 'He was home again' (line 57) describe Robert's meeting with the children, and his thoughts and feelings. They also prepare the reader for what is to happen.

- In the first three short paragraphs here, what things come as a surprise to Robert? What words does the writer use to signal Robert's 'disappointment'?

- What indications are there in these paragraphs that the girls have changed? Pick out the words and phrases that tell you this.

- What feelings does Robert have here? There are several different feelings.

- The girls are described as 'impulsive and affectionate' and Jenny as 'exciting', 'strong in all her feelings, intelligent, reflective', and as having 'moods of passionate devotion'. Which of these attributes do the girls show in what follows, and which are shown in ways that Robert does not expect?

- In the last of these paragraphs, Robert feels that he has 'lost most of his illusions' (line 53). Has he? Think about the words 'children ... never pretend' and 'the mere presence of the children was a pleasure. Nothing could deprive him of that. He was home again.' What happens in the rest of the story to dispel these ideas and feelings? How does he feel at the end?

5   The action of the story takes place over the next 55 lines from 'Jenny had got up and wandered away...' (line 58) to 'burst out again into helpless giggles' (line 112). It's these actions that shatter Robert's illusions.

- Robert thought that 'children ... never pretend'. Look at the words the girls use in these lines. What are they pretending here, and why is Robert 'shocked'?

- Look at the paragraph beginning 'The bitch, startled' (line 72). How are Snort's reactions the same as Robert's? Why has the writer shown the dog's reactions?

- Look at the paragraph beginning 'They tore at the man' (line 92). What feelings does Robert have here? What has changed?

- The next paragraph is the most violent. How does the writer suggest violence by the words and phrases he uses?

6 Look at the two paragraphs beginning 'Robert picked himself up' (line 113). What is Robert 'deeply shocked' by? What else does he feel? What has changed?

7 Robert thinks of their world as a 'primitive, brutal world' (line 119). Think about the description of the garden at the beginning. How does the action of straightening his tie reject the children's world? How has Robert himself changed from the beginning, therefore?

8 What 'game' do the children play with him next? Pick out the evidence. Robert thinks this is 'more like a game' (line 130), though. What does he mean, do you think?

9 When Mrs Quick and her friend arrive, they also have roles to play. What roles? Their attitude of 'All you children – amusing yourselves' (line 139) is plainly wrong in one sense. Robert is hardly amused. But can you see any way in which they are 'all children'?

10 In the paragraph beginning 'Kate and Jenny were sent to wash' (line 141) the girls take on another set of roles. What? Where does their father belong in this game?

11 In the next paragraph, 'And now ...' (line 147), Robert tries to adjust to a changed role for himself. How?

12 Why has the writer mentioned the case of the fourteen-year-old boy, in the next paragraph? What has it to do with what is happening?

13 Robert wants to 'escape' (line 155). From what? Find the evidence. What does he want to escape to? Think about his attitude to the garden at the beginning. How has he changed?

14 When Jenny is on the wall at the end, she is in 'a superior position' (line 172). She is, of course, higher up than Robert – what else? Why is this new?

15 Look at the last two paragraphs of the story.

- How does the writer show that Robert is uncertain about his daughter now?

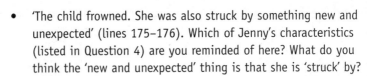

- 'The child frowned. She was also struck by something new and unexpected' (lines 175–176). Which of Jenny's characteristics (listed in Question 4) are you reminded of here? What do you think the 'new and unexpected' thing is that she is 'struck' by?

- 'She's growing up – and so am I' (lines 178–179). How is Jenny growing up, and how is Robert growing up, do you think?

Final thoughts

Robert's mood changes several times during the story. What do you think it is at the end?

There are a lot of references to games in the story. How have Robert and Jenny been forced to examine their roles in each other's lives during the story? How are these roles changing?

Questions

Foundation Tier

Compare the ways relationships between young and older people are shown in **Growing Up** and **Superman and Paula Brown's New Snowsuit**.

You should write about:

- the relationships in each story

- what the young people realise about the older people in each story

- what each writer wants readers to think about the young people and the older people in each story

- how the writers show the young and the older people through the ways that they write about them.

Higher Tier

In **Growing Up** and **Flight** the main characters learn things about themselves and others. What different things do they learn?

You should compare:

- what they learn about themselves and others
- the attitudes and feelings of the main characters
- how the writers structure their stories
- the language that the writers choose to use.

Ernest Hemingway

a Ernest Hemingway (1899–1961) was an American novelist and short story writer. Much of his writing is deliberately unsentimental.

The End of Something

g **Glossary**

trolling   fishing with a hook and line behind a boat

Read and revise

Read the story right through once, focusing on Nick's mood, and his feelings about Marjorie.

1. The first three paragraphs set the background to the story, but the connections between the place and the events in the story are never made explicit by the writer. The paragraphs make up about a fifth of the whole length, though, which suggests they have an important part to play in the story's design.

   • The story is called **The End of Something**, and is about something being over, becoming part of the past. Pick out the words and phrases in the first three paragraphs that suggest things belonging to the past, or being over.

   • There's a sense of loss at the end of the story, too. Pick out words and ideas that relate to loss, or being alone.

   • Something is stopped and destroyed at the end. Find all the suggestions you can of things stopping that were once active, or things being destroyed.

   • In the third paragraph there is nothing left of the mill except the 'broken white limestone of its foundations' (line 15). What is left at this point of the relationship between Nick and Marjorie?

   • Where Nick and Marjorie are rowing, the bottom 'dropped off' to 'dark water' (line 18). How can you relate these phrases to what happens, and to the mood of the story?

   Now you've worked through these questions, think about the importance of these paragraphs to the effect of the story. The details **symbolise** what is to happen, in a way – they set the tone for the story, by representing the events and the mood of what is to follow.

2 Look at the first conversation between Nick and Marjorie, from 'There's our old ruin (line 20)' to 'She loved to fish with Nick' (line 30).

- How do the first two things Marjorie says try to evoke the past, and something shared with Nick?

- Now look at Nick's replies. How has he responded to Marjorie's invitations?

- Marjorie's third statement is an invitation to imagination – romance, even. What is Nick's response?

- Nick's remark 'They aren't striking' (line 28) is negative, like much of what he says. Is Marjorie's reply, 'No', negative as well? Think of her interaction with Nick in the conversation, rather than what they mean about the fish.

- Hemingway repeats the phrase 'She loved to fish' (line 30), adding 'with Nick' the second time. What is the effect of the repetition? What does it tell you about Marjorie?

3 Now look at the next ten lines, up to 'the boat touched the shore' (line 39).

- Hemingway's writing is very spare – the sentences tend to be short, and there are very few comparisons, so where there is a comparison it tends to have a stronger effect. The effect of the minnows on the water is described as 'a handful of shot'. Why has the writer chosen this image to describe it? Think about the beginning of the story again.

- In the snatch of conversation here, how is Marjorie positive and Nick negative, and what does it say about their attitudes to each other?

- Marjorie 'did not reel in until the boat touched the shore' (line 39). What is she hoping for, until the last minute? How does this relate to the end of the story?

4 The next few paragraphs, up to 'Nick pulled the boat high up on the beach' (line 62), describes the way they lay the bait. Who is in control here? How do you know?

5 'What's the matter, Nick?' (line 63) brings the problem into the open. Why does Marjorie think there is a problem?

6 How does Nick's reply confirm that there is a problem? There are only three words in his reply. Look back over his words so far, noticing how few words he uses. What does this suggest about his mood and attitude?

7 What do their attitudes to eating show about Nick and Marjorie at this point?

8 Nick and Marjorie's final conversation runs from 'There's going to be a moon tonight' (line 78) to 'She was afloat in the boat on the water with the moonlight on it' (lines 106–107). This is where the end, which has been hinted at throughout, finally comes.

- Look at the paragraph beginning 'There's going to be a moon tonight' (line 78). Pick out the words and phrases that suggest change beginning to happen. How does this reflect what is taking place? What does Nick's attitude to this change seem to be?

- The moon symbolises the change here. There are four mentions of it in these lines. How does the progress of the moon mirror the course of the change that happens to Nick and Marjorie?

- When Nick is aggressive about Marjorie 'knowing everything' (line 84), Marjorie 'did not say anything'. Earlier, Nick's silence is seen as a rejection. Is this the same, do you think?

- What are Nick and Marjorie's physical positions in relation to each other during the conversation? Count how many times the writer mentions it. What is he conveying to the reader, do you think?

- This is their only really direct conversation. Up to now, the reader has had to infer Nick's emotions – they have not been stated. Here, though, he 'was afraid to look at Marjorie' (line 97). Why do you think he is afraid to look at her? Why has Hemingway not given his emotion directly until now?

9 Now look again at the last ten lines of the story (109–118).

- How do you think Nick feels about what has happened? What is the evidence for your view?

- How much does Bill know about what has happened? What has obviously taken place before Nick and Marjorie go fishing? What does this tell you about Nick?

- Bill is clearly wary of Nick. Why?

- '"Yes," Nick said, lying, his face on the blanket' (line 113). What are the two possible meanings of 'lying' here? Did Marjorie 'go all right'?

- What is the difference between Bill's attitude to eating and fishing and Nick and Marjorie's attitudes?

Final thoughts

This story appears to be very simply written, but there is a lot below the surface. Read the story again, noticing how Hemingway uses the setting of the story to match the events, and how he conveys moods and feelings without naming them explicitly.

Questions

Foundation Tier

The characters in **The End of Something** and **Growing Up** are involved in conflict. Write about the conflicts, and the ways the writers present them.

You should compare:

- the different kinds of conflict
- what you think the writers' purposes are
- the ways the stories are shaped, and the ways the writers use language
- your response to the stories.

Higher Tier

Several characters in the stories change their minds about things. Write about **The End of Something** and **one** other story from this collection, comparing characters and the ways they change.

Graham Swift

a — Graham Swift is a British novelist and short story writer. His work is often both dramatic and mysterious.

Chemistry

Read and revise

'Chemistry' in this story means both reactions between chemicals, and the 'chemistry' between people – the way people react with each other in often complex relationships. Read the story right through once, focusing on these 'chemistries'.

<u>1</u> The first paragraph sets up some key elements of the story.

- The close relationship between the boy and his mother and grandfather is at the heart of the story. How does the writer emphasise its closeness in the first four sentences? Look for particular words, phrases and repetitions.

- The natural setting is used throughout to echo the events. In the fourth sentence, 'We would go even in the winter ...' (line 4), what two natural changes are suggested? Changes in nature depend on chemistry too, of course.

- 'Grandfather, in his black coat and grey scarf, would walk to the far side to receive it' (lines 8–9). Look at the last paragraph of the story. What else from the opening is repeated in the final paragraph? Think what actions are being described.

- Look at the sentence beginning 'As it moved it seemed ... ' (line 13). What does this suggest about grandfather's motives throughout the story? What happens when one of the other two is finally 'beyond his reach'?

<u>2</u> The second paragraph, beginning 'the voyages were trouble-free', also contains an idea that informs the rest of the story. The sinking of the boat takes on several meanings.

- 'The voyages were trouble-free' when boy, Mother and Grandfather were together. The boat sank 'soon after Mother met Ralph' (line 22). How do these two events seem to be connected? Does the boy just mean literally 'at the same time' – and even if he does, what has been established in the reader's mind?

- There is an 'invisible cord' (line 15) which links Grandfather on one side with the Mother and child on the other. What happens when the launch sinks, therefore?

- 'You must accept it – you can't get it back – it's the only way' (lines 26–27). How does the writer make clear that Grandfather is not thinking simply about the loss of the boat? Think about who he appears to be talking to, and who he's actually talking to, and the Mother's reaction.

- The idea of accepting loss, and the change that goes with it, is very important in the story. With the help of the rest of the questions, you can trace it right through the story.

- 'You can't get it back – it's the only way' has several meanings. What losses occur before the action of the story, and during it? What 'only ways' are taken by people who suffer loss?

<u>3</u> Look at the next section, from 'It was some months after' (line 30) to 'the way Vera taught you' (line 41).

- How is it clear that the boy has not accepted Ralph?

- 'What do you know about being left alone' (line 37). Who has been and is 'left alone' in the story?

- Has the Grandfather accepted loss, and the necessity of not looking back? Find evidence for your answer.

- After 'the way Vera taught you' the narrative breaks off while the boy gives some background to the situation. Find the point where the story around the meal begins again.

<u>4</u> The next 35 lines (lines 42–76) give their history up to the father's death.

- Pick out all the suggestions in these lines of family continuity – things not changing – in looks and situations.

- How are the deaths of the father and Grandmother linked, in the boy's mind? What is the similarity between these two deaths (the way the boy imagines them) and an event earlier in the story?

- 'If I really believed Father was gone for ever – I was wrong' (lines 67–68). How was he wrong? When the mother holds the boy, is she accepting loss and change? What change (almost a chemical one) does she seem to fear?

<u>5</u> Read the next two paragraphs, beginning 'For about a year' (line 77).

- What is there in these lines that suggests happiness? Is it complete?

- What is there in these lines that suggests that the existence being described is unnatural, or unreal?
- What is it that destroys this existence?

6 Look at the next section, from 'Sometimes when Grandfather provoked' (line 90) to 'it means she really loves Ralph' (line 107). The complex relationships described here could well be described as 'chemistry' – the inter-relationship of elements. Pick out the words that liken this human chemistry to the chemistry of science.

7 When the boy's mother pulls him to her (line 119), the boy feels momentarily that nothing has changed. Look at the description of the garden beyond them. How is the course of nature being defied outside? What does it suggest about the boy's feeling inside the house?

8 The boy is mistaken about the decision his mother has made (lines 128–131). What does this show about him? What does the mother's decision show about her? Think about loss and acceptance.

9 Look at the next section, from 'I don't think Grandfather practised chemistry' (line 143) to 'with quiet self-absorption' (line 160).

- What do you think 'I learnt from Grandfather the fundamentals of chemistry' (line 146) means?
- What is there in the description of the shed that suggests that it is an unnatural place?
- What is wrong with grandfather? Think about the last phrase in the section, as well as the other things.

10 Grandfather says 'Anything can change' (line 163). Can he? How does the boy think about making things change?

11 When Grandfather talks about gold-plating (lines 177–179), he is not just thinking about metal – look how quickly he moves to 'What are we going to do?' What do you think he means by 'real gold' in human chemistry, and what only 'looked as if it was all gold'?

12 'Then I had a strange sensation' (line 191). What do you think the boy sees and thinks at this moment? There's something about family continuity, clearly. But what about 'every face is like this' and 'there is no end to anything'? Think about chemistry (as in biology), and the deaths in the story.

13 Look at the two sentences beginning 'All that autumn' (line 202). How is the natural background suggesting change now?

14 'She looked trapped and helpless' (line 210). The boy assumes she is 'trapped' helplessly by Ralph – but how else might she be 'trapped'?

15 'Death is a deceptive business' (line 219). What do you think the boy means by this? Think about all of the deaths mentioned in the story, and how they might be 'deceptive' in different ways.

16 Look at the paragraph which describes father's 'visit' (lines 231–241).

- Which two losses does the father link together?

- 'Don't you believe me?' is a challenge to the boy. How does the writer emphasise that it's a challenge – almost like a dare?

- Do you believe him? Does he accept loss and change?

17 Look at the paragraph beginning 'And then it was almost light' (line 242).

- Look at the description of the rain dashing against the window. What does the comparison, 'plunging under water', make you think of in the context of this story? How does this connect with what is happening at this moment in the story?

- When the ambulance arrives, the reader does not know who it is for. Work out how the writer keeps the reader guessing, by revealing the living people.

18 The next five paragraphs, from 'But she never did explain' (line 256) to 'Ralph's buying it' (line 279), describe the events immediately after Grandfather's death.

- The boy thinks that his mother should have 'confessed' (line 258), and wants to explain that 'suicide can be murder' (line 272). How do you think Grandfather died? Who does the boy blame for his death? Who do you blame?

- Look at the descriptions of nature on the day of Grandfather's funeral, and a week later. How has the weather changed? What does it suggest to you about the effect of Grandfather's death?

- You might think about 'gold', which is mentioned twice here, and look back to lines 177–179. 'Gold leaves' and 'a mock version' suggests something like Grandfather's gold-plating – not 'real gold' at all. The leaves on the rowan tree are 'all gold', though. Is there a 'gold' relationship here? And is the boy the right person to know what it is? Whatever your answers might be, it's clear that the writer is using both nature and 'chemistry' to make you reflect on the nature of the human relationships in the story.

- In the paragraph beginning 'And then after the funeral', what does the move to a new house remind you of, earlier in the story? What else here might make you think of continuity and change?

19 The boy thinks about 'how things don't end' (line 272) and 'though things change they aren't destroyed' (line 282). This is true of chemical elements, of course, but what else? Think about the lives, deaths and relationships in the story – and what happens in the last five lines of the story.

20 Look at the last seven lines of the story, from 'It was there' (line 282) to the end. What is there in these lines that reminds you of what has gone before? You should find a lot!

Final thoughts

This is a complex story, some of which is quite difficult to unravel – just like chemistry, really. Read the story again, now that you've done the detailed work. Focus on what the boy knows, and what he doesn't. The boy is 'barely ten', so the reader can perhaps understand things that he can't about relationships. The writer has created a narrator whom the reader can only partly believe.

You might also put together the way the writer uses nature throughout the story to make the reader reflect on the events.

? Questions

Foundation Tier

Compare **two** stories from the selection where characters find themselves in unusual situations.

You should write about:

- what the situations are, and why they are unusual
- what you learn about the characters from the different ways they deal with the situation
- how the writers show the unusual situations.

Higher Tier

In **Chemistry** and **Superman and Paula Brown's New Snowsuit** characters feel betrayed by others.

Compare how feelings of betrayal are shown in the two stories.

Leslie Norris

a

Leslie Norris is a Welsh poet and short story writer. He was born in Merthyr in 1926, and much of his work is about his childhood in Merthyr.

Snowdrops

Read and revise

Read the story through once, focusing on how the writer conveys the boy's age – his size, the way he thinks, what he understands and what he doesn't understand.

1 Look at the first paragraph. The focus of the story is set up here.

- Miss Webster and the snowdrops are the central things in the boy's mind during the story. How does the writer emphasise this in these five lines?

- The boy thinks about the flowers and Miss Webster during the story, but they are brought together strikingly at the end of the story. Read again the next to last paragraph (lines 188–204), noticing how the focus is on both.

- The boy tries to imagine what they are like. How is that answered at the end?

- He thinks of the flowers as 'frail and white' (line 5). Can you find echoes of these words in the next to last paragraph?

2 Look at the next 17 lines, from 'It was a very cold morning' (line 7) to 'safely locked outside the house' (line 24). More elements of the story are established here.

- 'It was a very cold morning' (line 7). Count how many times in these lines the cold is either mentioned directly or implied. Notice how many times it appears in the rest of the story as you work through it. Why do you think the writer wants the cold established in the reader's mind as the backdrop to this particular story? Keep thinking about this as you work through.

- The boy notices 'with wonder' the effect of the firelight on his brother. The boy observes closely what is around him throughout the story. Which sentence here best expresses this about him? You'll notice this characteristic again and again as you work through the story.

- How does the writer convey the boy's physical size here? Think about his height compared to objects, and the angle from which he sees things.

- Much of the story is written from the boy's point of view, but the writer doesn't try to use words that only a child would use. Enough childish words and phrases are used to create this effect, though. 'What he did was this' (line 12) is an example here. Can you find any other words like this in these lines? You'll notice more as you work through the story.

3 'But his mother coughed and looked sharply at the boy' (line 41). Why does she do this, and what is she trying to prevent?

4 'Edmund was very brave' (line 56). Different sorts of bravery are mentioned in the story. How is Edmund 'brave' here? Notice the other kinds of bravery in the story.

5 Look at the two paragraphs beginning 'It wasn't too bad' (line 57). What is the boy's mind on all the time here?

6 Look at the passage about the sandwiches (lines 75–88).

- The taste is 'incredibly new and marvellous' (line 79) to the boy. Glance at the penultimate paragraph to find an echo of this.

- Edmund explains that 'it tastes different when it's cold' (line 88). This is more evidence of the boy's innocence, but there is more going on here. The boy sees something differently here. What does he see differently at the end of the story?

7 Look at the paragraph beginning 'The children cheered and clapped' (line 98).

- What sort of bravery has Miss Webster shown?

- What is unusual about Miss Webster here?

8 Look at the paragraph beginning 'The boy drew a robin' (line 103).

- How does the boy know how to draw the robin? How is this typical of him?

- The boy hasn't noticed that the other children had finished. How is this typical of him?

- The robin stands 'bravely'. What does the word mean here, do you think? The writer describes the robin's song as being 'like threads of falling water' – an unusual choice of comparison. The writer is

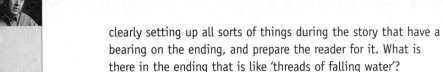

clearly setting up all sorts of things during the story that have a bearing on the ending, and prepare the reader for it. What is there in the ending that is like 'threads of falling water'?

- In the last three lines of the paragraph, what is unusual?

<u>9</u> The boy's story is about 'a wizard who could change himself into anything at all', but he can never finish it in his head. What change is completed in his head at the end of the story?

<u>10</u> 'Poor girl', said his mother' (line 135). How does the boy misunderstand this, and why?

<u>11</u> Look at the two paragraphs beginning 'But there was nobody about' (lines 150–163). What is unusual about Miss Webster's appearance and behaviour here? Are there any indications that some of the children understand what is happening, even though the boy doesn't?

<u>12</u> Look at the paragraph beginning 'He stood up with a sudden lightening of the heart' (line 168). The flowers are described as 'miraculous', 'pale and fragile' – all ideas which have occurred before, and appear again at the end. How is a connection made between the flowers and Miss Webster here? Look at how she is described.

<u>13</u> Look again at the next to last paragraph, beginning 'He squatted down to look at the snowdrops' (line 188). This is the conclusion to the story, in that he sees the snowdrops – but the other elements of the story come together here too.

- Look at the description of the snowdrops, and pick out the words which imply strength or bravery. How are they also described as weak?

- Now picture exactly what the snowdrops look like. How do they look similar to the position Miss Webster is in at the gate?

- The flowers clearly represent Miss Webster – so how do they help the reader to see her? How is she both brave and fragile?

- The boy knows now 'what snowdrops were'. What do you think this means?

Final thoughts

This seems a very simple story, but it is carefully crafted by the writer to produce an effective ending. Read through the story again, putting the elements you have worked on together.

The boy's best friend is Edmund Jenkins, and he is mentioned throughout the story. Do you think the relationship has relevance in the ending?

❓ Questions

Foundation Tier

In both **Snowdrops** and **Growing Up** the main characters learn something important.

Compare the way this is shown in the two stories.

Write about:

- what the characters learn, and how they learn it
- how the writers show the characters' thoughts and feelings by the ways they write
- differences between the stories.

Higher Tier

Compare the ways characters' thoughts and feelings are shown in **Snowdrops** and in **one** other story from the Anthology.

Write about:

- what makes the characters think and feel the way they do
- similarities and differences between the characters
- how the writers reveal the characters' thoughts and feelings.

Comparing short stories

The examination questions on the stories in the *Anthology* will ask you to write about two stories, and to compare them. When you're thinking about the individual stories in the selection, and especially when you're revising them before the exams, it's a good idea to think about them together. Some of the stories are quite similar to each other, either in what they are about or in the way that they're written, but at the same time some are very different. Even those that are alike in subject might be very different in style, and you might be asked about this too. This section looks at two stories that could easily be compared, though you might be asked about any combination. The suggestions are presented in note form – the sort of notes you might make in preparing for your answer. You'll need to add plenty of evidence from the text for a full answer.

Two stories which could be looked at together and compared are **Flight** by Doris Lessing and **Your Shoes** by Michèle Roberts. One way to look at them together is to think about the content, such as the feelings, attitudes and ideas in the stories, then at the style – how the writers have expressed their ideas. The exam questions often ask you to explore the stories in this way, too, though you certainly don't have to be rigid in following this approach. Here are some of the things that might occur to you when look at these two stories.

Content

- *Situations* similar – older person wants to restrain younger. Grandfather / grandchild in **Flight**, mother / daughter in **Your Shoes**. Young people ready to leave.

- Older people's feelings and attitudes similar – both hurt, both selfish. Both resent the actions of the young.

- Stories are different too, e.g. the endings, though both result from older person's attitude. Grandfather accepts, forces himself to change; mother will not change, locked into grief. Young people respond differently. Granddaughter in **Flight** calms her grandfather and loves him, as shown by distress at end; daughter in **Your Shoes** apparently does not, though not shown.

Style

- *Tone* emotional in both – shown differently. **Flight** uses third person – we see old man objectively, and from daughter's and granddaughter's point of view. **Your Shoes** uses first person, and letter form. Emotions and events through mother's eyes only – have to infer things about central figure which are given directly in **Flight**. Present tense – unfolds dramatically.

- *Symbolism* used in both stories and titles. Pigeon in **Flight** = granddaughter. The old man wants 'his favourite' to stay, but at the end deliberately releases her. In **Your Shoes** Mother wants to restrain daughter – shoes represent her: 'I locked the wardrobe door on those rebellious shoes'. At the end 'safe and warm' with the mother, in her mind. Dramatic climax in both stories depends on central symbol.

Structuring a prose response

When you set about responding to a question in the examination, it's important to take some time to plan your work. In this section there's an example of a plan for a particular question – but remember that there may be a number of other ways to plan a successful answer. As well as questions that name particular stories, there will also be one question which allows you to choose any two stories you like. Suppose, for example, that the question in the exam was:

Compare two stories where characters face difficult situations.

You should write about:

- what the difficulties are
- how the characters deal with the difficulties
- what you think the writers want to say, and how they say it
- how you respond to the situations, and how you think the writers make you respond in this way.

You could choose almost any of the stories to answer this question. If, for example, you decided to use the same two stories as we've looked at in Comparing Stories – **Flight** and **Your Shoes** – how would you go about it? A table has been provided to help you to think along the right lines. One way of structuring a response is simply to follow the bullets one by one, if these are offered – but you don't *have* to do it this way. You *do* have to cover what they suggest at some point in your writing, though, so it's important to look carefully at what they're asking.

Looking at the bullet points in this question, it's clear that the first two are asking something about content, and the second two about style. The two are obviously very closely related, and you might not want to divide them in this way, but let's suppose that your structure simply followed the bullets. The plan, with a little detail to indicate what you're going to write about in each section, might look something like the one opposite.

This is a pretty detailed plan, but when you go into the exam you should know the stories so well that you could write a plan like this without having to open your *Anthology* at all. You should probably only have to refer to it to look at some details. You might well think of a lot more to say as you write, which is fine, but if you stick to the outlines of your plan it will help you to answer the question effectively. Remember – you must give evidence from the texts to back up the points and comments that you make. Notice that in the plan the words 'perhaps' and 'possibly' are used. These are all the kinds of things you could write, and when the question asks 'how you respond' it means just that – your own, individual, response. In the end, the examiner wants to know what you think.

Flight	Your Shoes
1 What the difficulties are	
Outlines the grandfather's reluctance to let the girl go / the girl's problems dealing with her grandfather, and her distress when he lets her go.	The mother's problems coming to terms with her daughter's flight / the daughter's reasons for leaving – possibly.
2 How the characters deal with the difficulties	
Grandfather's anger / spite, appeal to daughter, overcoming by recognising inevitability, the release; girl's manipulation of the old man, but distress when she realises the significance of his action.	Mother's self-justification / criticism of daughter / madness.
3 What you think the authors want to say, and how they say it	
About problems of letting young people grow up and leave home. Story in third person lets us see grandfather's motives clearly – use of pigeon as symbol for girl and her release – flight in title.	About problems of letting young people grow up and leave home. First-person narrative to convey mother's feelings and her increasing madness as story unfolds – change on last page and attitude to shoes – shoes as symbol and in title.
4 How you respond to the situations, and how you think the authors make you respond in this way	
Perhaps eventual sympathy for the grandfather, and realising that the girl is not heartless – after his 'gesture of self-command', the girl's distress and the author's use of light / shade / symbolism at the end.	Perhaps horror at the woman's condition at the end – created by the lapse into clear madness on the last page, the disjointed nature of the last few sentences, the use of symbolism at the end.

Sample answers and commentaries

In this section you will find three responses to the Higher Tier sample question which follows the story **Flight** by Doris Lessing. The writers were all Year 10 students preparing for the examination. Their work was marked by a senior examiner and graded A, C and E respectively. The examiner's comments, showing why these grades were awarded, follow the answers themselves. The question was:

In **Flight**, Doris Lessing uses pigeons to represent something else. Write about how she does this, and how the author of one other story in the *Anthology* uses the same technique.

You should write about:

- the things the authors have used, and what they represent
- why the authors have chosen to use these particular things
- how the authors show that these things are meant to represent something else
- what the authors gain from using this technique.

William (Grade A)

In the stories **Flight** and **Your Shoes**, the writers express many ideas through the objects in them (pigeons in **Flight** and white training shoes in **Your Shoes**). These objects enhance the stories' plots and enable the writers to bring out the history and surroundings of the main characters.

In **Flight** the pigeons represent the granddaughter Alice; we see a comparison between the two in the way the light shines off them:
   'The sunlight broke on their grey breasts.'
   'Her hair fell down her back in a wave of sunlight.'
These lines show us how the sunlight is used to link the granddaughter with the pigeon. The linkage shows us the way the pigeons are used to express how the granddaughter has grown up and is now leaving home.

In **Your Shoes**, the trainers could represent two people in the story, the daughter who has run away or the narrator's mother. The daughter is joined with the trainers in their whiteness, for white symbolises purity and cleanliness (which is why it is worn for weddings to symbolise virginity in the bride) because the narrator is wishing to cleanse her daughter through the shoes. This is because her daughter is no longer a member of the virgin club and so has had sex which her mother, the narrator, was trying to protect her from. She may also wish to purify her daughter through the trainers, for in the story it is mentioned that the daughter may have to take up prostitution so that she can feed herself, and the narrator of course does not want this for her special young innocent little girl. The mother may also be trying to mould her daughter through the trainers for they are everything she wants them to be, well presented, clean and, most of all, white (a virgin again) and the mother desperately wants this for her daughter.

The trainers could represent the grandmother due to the fact that they are a comfortable, well-fitting shoe and the grandmother always used to wear shoes that were the wrong size and had a high heel to them:
    'Rows of high heels, all of them too small for her.'
The comparison comes in the contract between these shoes and the trainers and how the grandmother's shoes, are so tight, causing corns and bunions, whereas the white trainers are so light and easy to walk in. When the narrator is talking about her mother she calls her a tart, referring to the way she used to dress and act, which makes her like the daughter, and the narrator makes the same comparison:
    'My mother was like you.'
This line seems to sum up how the mother / narrator thinks of both her relatives, and so links all three (the white trainers, the daughter and the grandmother) together.

In **Flight**, Lessing shows the pigeons as a symbol of Alice by contrasting one image against another, for example:
    'A young pigeon, the light gleaming on its breast.'
This image, along with one of Alice walking up the street with Steve with the light glowing from her face shows us the similarities of the two again with a good use of light.

The trainers in **Your Shoes** are showing us the mother's need for order in the way she continually moves them around the daughter's room, always keeping them neatly displayed together. The mother's need for order probably comes from her strict and non-truant upbringing as a child, which could also have led to her becoming a school teacher due to her need of order portrayed to her by her parents which came due to their strict upbringing. In this factor the mother feels guilty due to her not bringing her child up correctly, and we can see this in the way she sucks on and cradles the shoes. In this she could be looking for a way of trying to explore the bonding that comes through breast feeding, which the mother had been and the daughter not, and so the narrator is looking for that bond between mother and daughter. She is also trying to make her daughter into a baby again so that she cannot make any decisions for herself and completely relies on her again. On the other hand the narrator could just be demented and rocking for comfort like a baby does but, whichever way you look at it, she is trying to draw comfort from somewhere.

In **Flight**, the writer Lessing gets the idea of growing up across to her readers through the ideas of Alice being the last of many and the grandfather wishing to hold on to her so that he can protect her again. A similar thing is happening in **Your Shoes** – the writer through the relationship between the three ladies and the shoes is venturing into the ideas of teenage life and the relationships that a child needs with all his or her relatives. In both stories the writers thicken and enhance their plots through using the symbols, for they can explore ideas that would not be possible without them. For example, in **Your Shoes** and **Flight**, both symbols are attached to movement – the homing pigeon can fly and you use trainers to walk, both viable means of getting away from your parents and elders. This is portraying the need to spread your wings and get away when you are older; both are in different situations but both are the same.

Commentary

William's response to the question begins very directly, identifying the symbols in the two stories quickly and focusing on the writers' purposes. The identification of the pigeon with the granddaughter is made succinctly, with two well-chosen quotations for illustration, and an explanation. William then offers two readings of the shoes in Michèle Roberts's story, exploring the choice of white as a colour for the shoes because of its associations, and anchoring this firmly in the text. Exploration and development, which are the hallmark of this response, are evident in the language here: *'The trainers could represent ...'*, *'She may also wish to purify her daughter through ...'* The possibilities of the choice of whiteness are closely explored and analysed before William moves to consider the shoes as symbols for the grandmother, for different reasons.

One of the Assessment Objectives refers to comparisons 'within and between texts', and William compares effectively the two types of shoe in the story, and the people they represent, illustrating this with *'My mother was like you'*. He then builds this – *'This line seems to sum up how ... '* – into a sensitive insight into the author's purposes and methods.

William then compares this multiple use of imagery by Roberts with Lessing's use – *'by contrasting one image against another'* – and analyses a detail of presentation in Lessing's 'good use of light'.

Returning to **Your Shoes** – the story he is clearly more interested in – William embarks on a sensitive and close interpretation of some of the meanings expressed by the shoes and how the mother treats them. Even after a convincing view is offered, William gives another interpretation which is equally arguable in context, and then makes a clear evaluation of what can be said: '*On the other hand, the narrator could just be demented and rocking for comfort like a baby does but, whichever way you look at it, she is trying to draw comfort from somewhere.*'

William then compares the way the two writers convey '*the idea of growing up*' to their readers through the symbols they use, recognising the centrality of the symbols in the design and effect of the stories – a convincing response to the final prompt. He gives a further analytical example of this in the ways that '*both symbols are attached to movement*'.

This is a most impressive and enthusiastic response, offering a wide range of interpretations while remaining firmly rooted in the text, and analysing writers' choices, methods and purposes effectively. Much more is written about **Your Shoes** than **Flight**, perhaps reflecting the range of possibilities which the candidate sees, but this does not reduce the mark. This response deserves a mark in the A* band.

Anthony (Grade C)

In **Flight** the symbol is the pigeons and because they leave and fly away they represent the old man's granddaughter; but as the pigeons will be coming back he realises that she also will. At first he doesn't want to lose either his granddaughter or his pigeons, 'He deliberately held out his wrist for the bird to take flight, and caught it again at the moment it spread its wings'. He wants the bird to feel freedom and realises it is his to give or take. With the granddaughter he just wants her to stay at home with him permanently.

In **Your Shoes** by Michèle Roberts the symbols are shoes. When the writer is clearing out her mother's clothes she noticed that the shoes were badly misshapen, 'all of them moulded to the shape of her poor feet'. So on the way home from there she bought her daughter a pair of new shoes, 'white trainers, you see, I know what you like'. The writer thinks she knows her daughter and by buying the shoes is trying to mould her how she would like her daughter to be.

In **Flight** the writer has chosen to use the pigeons as a symbol because they fly away but do come back. She uses pigeons because they always come back, as the old man wants the granddaughter to do. In **Your Shoes** the writer uses the new shoes because they have not been worn and are pure, as the person telling the story would like her daughter to be. The phrase 'moulded to the shape' shows that he mother of the person telling the story tried to mould herself as the narrator is trying to mould her daughter.

In **Flight** the writer shows the pigeons are symbols because the old man does not want the birds to go, 'clenched in the pain of loss', as he does not want his granddaughter to go. Eventually he says, 'Now you can go' which is referring to his favourite pigeon, but also to his granddaughter, whom he is letting go and marry the postmaster's son. In **Your Shoes**, the writer shows the shoes as being symbols because at the end of the story the narrator is holding them to her breast and holding close to her, while rocking them 'like her mother never rocked me'. The text also says 'Let me hold her while you cry', which shows the narrator thinking of the shoes as her baby.

In **Flight** the author uses the pigeons as they are easier to show going and coming back than humans. The author also compares the two with nature: 'her long legs repeated the angle of the frangipani stems' and 'the light gleaming on its breast'. In **Your Shoes** the author gains from using shoes as a symbol because the narrator's mother tried to mould herself to her shoes, as the narrator is trying to mould the daughter as she would like her to be.

Commentary

Anthony begins by locating the device of the pigeons in **Flight** and explaining how they represent the granddaughter. He interprets the symbol in terms of the pigeon's desire for freedom and the old man's power over it, which he wants to exercise over the girl too, and carefully supports a comment with a relevant quotation. Shoes are identified as the symbol in **Your Shoes**, and he implies that they represent the daughter, though this is not clearly explained.

Anthony has chosen to use the prompts as a structure for his response, and now moves on to the reasons that these things have been chosen. A convincing reason is given for each choice, though neither adds much to what is said about the symbols in the first paragraph. However the connection between the narrator's mother and her own relationship with her daughter is more explicitly linked to the idea of being *'moulded to the shape'*.

The way Doris Lessing shows that the pigeon represents the girl is explained well, with two effective references to the text. The use of the shoes is shown too, with some sense of development, *'the text also says ...'* beginning a comment about *'the narrator thinking of the shoes as her baby'*.

Anthony closes with two convincing suggestions of the 'gains' of using the pigeon in **Flight**, both of which break new ground, though the comment on **Your Shoes** is a repetition from earlier.

Overall, the use of the prompts as structure perhaps held Anthony back a little, producing repetition where more material could have been explored. However, there is sustained focus on the task, effective use of textual details to support argument, and features of the authors' methods explained, and explored, a little. A mark well up in the C band is justified.

Lily (Grade E)

In the story **Flight**, Doris Lessing uses pigeons which represent the old man's granddaughter. He uses the pigeons to remind him of his granddaughter who he still treats as if she is still a little girl. She wants to move away and have a life of her own, but the grandfather doesn't want to let her go as she is his last granddaughter that hasn't left. He finds it hard that she is leaving so he threatens to tell her mum; he will be probably thinking that she is going to give in to him but she doesn't care. The granddaughter says that she will always come back to visit, just as the pigeons do when they fly – they always come back to the place they call home. When the old man is holding the pigeon in his hand, and is going to let the pigeon free, he catches it as soon as it is going to take flight; this shows that he wants to let go of his granddaughter but he can't, she means too much to him.

In the story **Your Shoes**, Michèle Roberts uses a pair of shoes which represent the mother's daughter. The mother treats the shoes as if they were the daughter; she holds them close to her and has them sitting beside each other; she has even tied the shoe laces together so they won't get separated or lost and washed and ironed the laces so they are perfect. The mother wants her daughter to be like the shoes, pure and a virgin. The pigeons are used to represent the granddaughter as they fly away and come back, and so will the granddaughter. In both stories they don't want their daughters to grow up too fast.

English Literature: Prose

Commentary

Lily begins her response by locating the feature she has been asked about in **Flight** – *'Doris Lessing uses pigeons which represent the old man's granddaughter.'* She then explains why Alice wants to leave, and why her grandfather wants to keep her. She really just tells a bit of the story here, though with a purpose, as she reminds the reader by writing about Alice coming back *'just as the pigeons do'*. She then generalises about the old man's feelings, referring to the details of his behaviour with the pigeon.

Dealing with **Your Shoes**, she again locates the symbol, and identifies it by referring to the details of the way the mother behaves with the shoes. There's explanation here, too: *'The mother wants her daughter to be like the shoes, pure and a virgin'*, and an explanation of a reason for using the pigeons. Lily ends with a simple comment about a similarity between the stories.

This response does not fit neatly into a mark band. There are flashes of clear explanation of devices in the texts, which would suggest a mark in C, but the response is brief and, even within its length, lapses into narrative. There's some awareness of authors at work, though implicitly, some generalisations, and some use of text. The best fit is in the E band, though the flashes of higher skills push it to the top of that band.

Glossary

The following technical words are used in some of the questions about individual stories or poems.

alliteration the deliberate repetition of initial consonant sounds to gain a particular effect

ambiguous something which can be interpreted in more than one way

assonance the deliberate repetition of vowel sounds to gain a particular effect

blank verse verse without rhyme, but with a regular rhythm

emotive appealing to, arousing or expressing emotion

end-stopped lines lines of verse which end with a full stop

epigraphs a quotation at the beginning of a poem, which usually suggests its theme

half-rhyme words in which the consonants rhyme rather than the vowels

iambic pentameter a line of verse with five beats, which fall on the second syllable of each pair

imagery language rich in metaphor and simile

irony the use of words to express something other than the literal meaning – usually the opposite, in fact

metaphor an image which makes an implied comparison by stating that something is the thing it resembles, e.g. 'The icicles were glittering diamonds in the sun'

narrator the person or voice who is telling the story

onomatopoeia the sound of words matching the sound being described

paradox a statement which apparently contradicts itself

persona a created character

personification a device whereby an abstract concept or non-living thing is represented as having human characteristics, e.g. 'Old Father Time'

refrain a recurring phrase or lines at the end of each stanza of poetry, like a chorus

rhyme scheme the way rhymes within a poem are organised

rhyming couplets two lines following one another which rhyme

rhyming triplet a unit of three lines of verse that rhyme

simile a comparison between two things, using 'like' or 'as'

sonnet a poem of fourteen lines, usually ending with a rhyming couplet

stanza a division of a poem in which the lines are arranged in a pattern of metre and rhyme, usually recurring

structure how the author has organised his / her work. In poetry, this may simply mean the stanza, though it will reflect the progression of thought too; in prose fiction, it is how the author has shaped his story

symbol something used to stand for or represent something else

syntax grammatical arrangement of words

vocabulary simply the words used